ASTROLOGY

LAL

By

D.P. SAXENA

Ranjan Publications
16, Ansari Road, Darya Ganj, New Delhi-110002 (India)

Published by :
RANJAN PUBLICATIONS
16, Ansari Road, Darya Ganj,
New Delhi-110002 (India)
Ph : 91-11-23278835, 23282998

ISBN : 81-88230-15-4

Edition : 2019

Price : ₹ 150 /-

Printed at : Harsh Printer Delhi

Contents

Preface

The Lal Kitab is a great work of our times written by one who happened to live amongst us. It is a treatise on astropalmistry with astrological remedies. In other works on palmistry we find names of lines, mounts and marks etc., after the names of planets and there ends their astrology. Lal Kitab after naming the mounts etc., after the names of planets goes much further. Palmistry is explained in astrological terms. This work would have attained the status of a great classic but for its script which is Persian and which finds very few students today. I have tried to remove this handicap by stating in English what has been written in Urdu. The original text in Urdu was studied and copious notes were taken. This work is based on those notes. The Lal Kitab is astro-palmistry. In the present book I have tried to restrict myself to its astrological part.

It may be stated at the outset that some of the astrological concepts and assumptions are quite new to the current astrological thought. A brief reference to them has been made in the opening part of the book under the heading *Introduction*. This is with a view to inform the reader that the astrology provided in the book is not identical with the astrology we know.

In the second chapter Twelve Houses of the Horoscope the nomenclature of the houses, as found in the book, has been given. How different planets behave in different houses has also been discussed in this chapter. There is the question of aspects which has been dealt with at proper place. There is, however, some secret relationship or mutual understanding between the planets which is called the Yoga drishti of planets in the Lal Kitab. This aspect has also been discussed in the same chapter under a sub heading "More about the houses". Here I have also given the commodities etc., governed by the houses.

In the 3rd chapter "The Planets" some preliminary information is given about the planets in general like their classifications etc. New concepts of matching planets, equivalent planets and comrade planets have also been given here. The things relating to planets and combination of planets have also been given here.

The third chapter is a discussion about the planets in general. This is again slightly different from the current thought in some respects. The information regarding the nature and classification of planets provides an interesting reading. Some general discussion is there about planetary aspects (normal), Yoga drishti of planets, their affliction in certain houses and the articles and relatives signified by the planets. Besides this, there is a discussion about each individual planet in each house and remedies suggested for his bad effects in various houses. This portion has been marked as chapter 4.

In the 4th chapter "More about the planets" there is a brief discussion about each individual planet and suitable remedies for its bad results in each house.

The Lal Kitab has divided the human brain in 42 divisions and these divisions are associated with the houses of the horoscope. This aspect has been dealt with in chapter 5. This is perhaps the most important part in as much as it equips us with handling the problem child and understanding the real man/woman/child in the native.

The 6th chapter throws light on an important aspect of human life. This is the *Rina Pitri* or the parental curse. How to identify the person who has cursed the native and his family and suitable remedies to ward off the curses pertaining to various houses have also been given.

There are cases where normal remedies for evil effects defy solution. This is due to some curses not only on the native but on his/her entire family. This aspect has been given in chapter No.6 under the heading *Rina Pitri.*

The 7th chapter provides information regarding sicknesses and diseases which have not only become common these days; but also too complicated to be easily identified. In fact there is need to provide more such subjects but the same could not be done because of the paucity of space. Evil of the curse has been given. I have discussed in brief how the chart should be examined in the cases of sickness and the illnesses signified by the planets.

Chapter 8 deals with the precautions required for handling day-to-day problems like going to new residential premises, selection of brides or bridegrooms etc..

Chapter 9 lists the various remedial measures of Lal Kitab for various planetary ills. In fact this is the most important part of **Lal Kitab** as the book has drawn admirers on account of these remedial measures.

Here the book virtually ends but to make the book easier I have added some hints for prediction which may be found useful by the readers in putting their theoretical knowledge to practical application. This has been done under chapter 10.

In the last chapter called the "Critical Appreciation" the author has taken liberty to express his views on the book and its astrological philosophy.

– D.P. SAXENA

1

Introduction

Lal kitab needs no formal introduction. It is popular amongst neophytes and masters of astrology equally. The people in general who frequent the astrologers are enamoured of the remedial measures of Lal Kitab and the astrologers who suggest them take pride in them. The measures are too simple to be explained in detail and too typical to be understood by an intelligent human being. Whatever be the facts they are quite effective and cannot be just given up for their simplicity. Rather they bring credit to him who suggests them.

On the face of it Lal Kitab is an important treatise on palmistry and astrology. Ordinarily the palmists talk of mounts and lines Sun, Moon and Mars etc., but it is in Lal Kitab only that we come across the birth charts of the natives having twelve houses and all the planets (earliest known nine planets) posited there. Rules of predictions are also very much like those enunciated in astrology. Despite all this, the astrology of Lal Kitab is different from astrology we know of, be it eastern, western or of any origin.

Lal Kitab is essentially a palmistry. The astrological contents that are added to it are to reflect the findings of a palmist or rather to corroborate it. The palm has been divided into 12 parts just as the natural Zodiac is divided into twelve signs like Aries, Taurus etc. Some types of shapes have been allotted to planets. These shapes wherever they exist on palm are supposed to be occupying particular houses of the birth chart. These signs represent the planets they are allotted to. Thus we have the twelve houses and the nine planets posited in the chart having twelve houses. The astrological chart is ready on the basis of the palm. They are often different from the birth charts prepared on astrological principles. The authenticity of astrological charts is to be corrected by the chart prepared from palm imprints. How charts are made from the palm is not our subject here. We propose only to discuss and deal with astrological contents of the book.

Whatever be the system or method of preparing the chart has ascendant or the lagna and the other twelve houses numbered serially. Though they are the 12 signs of the Zodiac the signs have no significance in the chart. For signs, we may say, each horoscope is to be treated just like the horoscope of Kala Purusha, that is, house No.1 should be considered as identical with Aries in all cases. As Sun is exalted in Aries and debilitated in Libra, we say that Sun is exalted in Lagna and debilitated in the 7th house. The lordship of the houses will also go likewise. Mars is always the lagna lord and Venus the 7th lord.

In the palm we talk of lower Mars and upper Mars. In Lal Kitab's astrology we have two Mars, one a malefic or bad Mars and the other a benefic *or* a kind of good Mars. This is one peculiarity of Lal Kitab's astrology. Both the Mars have their own properties.

As regards the comparative power of the planets it is the same as given in classical texts; but at the same time we come across the concept of equivalent planets. Mercury for instance, is considered to be equivalent to Sun in power of giving results.

We have a concept of blind or sleeping planets and blind or sleeping houses in Lal Kitab. The planets are supposed to have an aspect of some houses and affect the results of those houses. In Lal Kitab if the aspecting planet has no planet in the aspected house the aspecting planet becomes a blind planet himself. It may be pertinent to note that the aspect of the planet is not the same in each house. Sun, if posited in house 2, shall not aspect the 8th house but the 6th house only and if 6th house is unoccupied Sun becomes blind. In short it is the house that grants aspect to the planet. The house is blind if it has no planets in it. This is the concept in astrology also. We call that house as weak.

There is also a concept of the artificial planets. A group of two planets together form one particular artificial planet or a substitute of these planets. Sun and Venus together form one artificial Moon. Likewise there are artificial planets for each of the planets including the nodes Rahu and Ketu.

There is also a concept of sacrificial goats. If, suppose, Sun is afflicted by Saturn the effects of Sun shall be affected. This will not affect the effects of any other planet like Mars, Mercury or Rahu etc. According to Lal Kitab the affliction of Sun shall be passed on to Ketu. In other words the affliction would affect the results of Ketu. The affliction of Saturn would likewise affect the results of Rahu and Ketu. As these two planets form one artificial Venus, the results of Venus will be spoilt. The wife of the native may die or suffer from miseries and troubles. It may be brought on record that such effects have actually been noticed although Saturn does not represent wife nor he is the significator of wife. Such results do need a deep research and the results are likely to enrich our astrology.

We have a basic assumption that a planet gives the results of the houses of his lordship and those of the house occupied by him. He may, according to some, also offer the results of house or houses of which he is the natural significator although we have our own reservations yet the planet in Lal Kitab can give results of any house by applying suitable remedies. This is a revolutionary concept and really needs deep research work like the assumption of sacrificial goats referred to above.

These are some of the special features of Lal Kitab's astrology. They may look strange but it should be remembered that the basis of astrology in Lal Kitab is palmistry. Some of these features are useful in suggesting remedies. The concept of artificial planets particularly is of great help in remedies against planetary ills. Mercury is an enemy of Jupiter. If Mercury afflicts Jupiter we may try to help Jupiter because the group of Jupiter and Rahu together is an artificial Mercury. If Jupiter is propitiated Mercury shall lose half of his strength and Jupiter shall become extra strong. In case Jupiter afflicts Mercury we should propitiate Venus because Sun and Venus constitute Jupiter. By strengthening Venus we shall be increasing power of Mercury (Venus is Mercury's friend) and decreasing the power of affliction of Jupiter.

2

The Twelve Houses of the Horoscope

There are twelve signs in the natural Zodiac and 12 houses in the horoscope. All affairs of human life are divided into 12 classes and each class of affair is in the domain of one or the other house of the chart.

Out of the 12 houses the first house or the lagna is the most important of them all. Being the first house all the subsequent houses stand in relation to it. Every thing depends upon the strength or otherwise of this house. Lal Kitab states that the house is the house of struggle between Maya and Jiva or the soul and matter. In other words it is the house of struggle to get liberation from the shakles of Maya. It is the throne of the ruler. The achievements or failures of the native depend largely upon this house. In Lal Kitab this house also stands for education, intelligence and longevity. It says इल्म आयु घर पहले से (education, intelligence and longevity from house No.1). Mars is the ruler of this house. Sun is the natural significator. In fact Sun represents the human soul and vitality in the physical body. Planet posited in house No.1 aspects the planets in house No. 7 and unburdens itself to some extent provided the house No. 7 is occupied and not vacant. If this house is vacant the planets in house No. 1 become inert. This is also true if the lagna is not occupied. The lagna house becomes inactive or weak. This house has a relationship with house No. 11. If the latter is unoccupied the planet in lagna gives good results. If there are two or more planets in lagna Venus becomes the judge to decide about the nature of results. In other words Venus gets importance if there are two or more planets in the lagna, incidently. House No. 2, is the Dharmasthana or the place of worship. Venus is its ruler. It is but natural that our own deeds or misdeeds come to play their part in the struggle for liberation.

House No.2 stands as the Dharmasthana or the place of worship. It also has the portfolios of wealth, education, honour and mind. This is the house that stands for the fruits of the Karmas or the deeds and misdeeds of the native. Here is the seat of Jupiter the Jagat Guru or the preceptor of the world at large. House No.9 is considered to be the ocean of Karmas. It is from house No.9 that the winds laden with water of the Karmas rise and pour it on house No.2. For good results of house No.2 the house No.8 should be vacant or unoccupied. The results are likely to be better if house No.2 is also vacant. This may appear strange but every thing becomes clear if we go by the assumptions of Lal Kitab. Planets in house No.2 are aspected by the planets in house No.8 (not vice versa) and the planets in house 2 aspect the planets in house No.6. If houses 2, 6 and 8 are all occupied the poison of house No.8 shall be transferred to house No.6 through the agency of the aspect of the planets in house No.2. If houses 2 and 8 are both vacant there is no question of compounding the troubles of 6th house.

House No.2 gets its strength from house No.4. Wherever there is a severe onslaught of misfortunes from house No.9 due to the weakness of Dharmasthana or the Jagatguru or Venus, house No.4 comes to rescue. In times of adversities we should look towards the strength of 4th house, its lord and natural significator or Karaka Moon who stands for mother as well as mortality and mind. Perhaps mother's blessings may help the native tide over his/her difficulties.

Lal Kitab refers to house No.3 as the कूच का वक्त, राहे रवानगी or the time of exit from this world and the gateway of exit. In other words we come to know about the time of death and its causes. As illness is one of the routine ways of exit we have to judge the illness and diseases from this house. This is an inauspicious and malefic house that way.

Malefics in Dusthanas or inauspicious houses are normally considered to be a good placement. According to Lal Kitab the placement of sinners i.e. Rahu and Ketu in house No.3 is horrible. It is said that even if they are not able to bring about the end itself they shall be competent to bring about death-like position. This may happen when house 3 is occupied by Rahu or Ketu and houses 6 and/or 8 by malefics. In adversities this house gets strength from 12th house even though the planets in 12th house are enemies of the planets in the 3rd house. In a hypothetical case let us assume that Ketu occupies house No.3 and Mars is posited in house No.12. Mars is an enemy of Ketu; but in emergencies Mars will always help Ketu despite his enmity. Ketu shall have no ill effects upon the native. Likewise Jupiter in the 3rd house and Mercury, his enemy, in 12th house will not be able to cause any harm. On the other hand there will be all round happiness and prosperity. If the houses are occupied by two or more planets we have to assess the harm, if any, in respect of each planet and then draw our final conclusions. Rahu and Venus in 12th house normally bring about death of the partner – wife or husband – in 24th/25th year of the native. If Saturn occupies the 3rd house simultaneously Rahu will not be able to play his mischief. Saturn will help Venus.

Mercury is the lord of 3rd house, Mars its natural significator and Rahu shall have the dignity of exaltation.

House No.4 is the period of childhood and the prenatal period. It also covers the old age. Moon is the lord and natural significator of this house. It is a well known assumption that Moon is strong by night. Similar is the position of other planets in this house. They are strong by the night and also when there is some trouble.

Jupiter gets exalted here. No planet gives bad effects to the affairs of this house if Moon does not occupy any of the house No.1, 4, 7 or 10. Even the rank malefics like Rahu and Ketu become benefics for this house if Moon does not occupy any of the quadrangular houses. The bad effects of planets in house No.4 are transferred to the affairs of the house occupied by Saturn.

For the pre-natal period if any of Jupiter, Sun, Mars or Mercury is in 4th house the child will be safe and healthy in mother's womb before birth and even Rahu or Ketu would not be able to spoil that.

House No.5 is the house of progeny and the future of the native. How shall the native fare in the world can be known from house No.5. About the welfare of children also we have to judge the same house. So long as Jupiter is in good position there shall be peace and prosperity. This means that Jupiter should be benefic by his placement and position in the annual progressed charts. If houses 6 and/or 1 0 are afflicted the articles connected with the planet inimical to the planet in 5th house should be kept under ground in the house. If house No.8 is also afflicted the articles should be kept under ground in the ancestral house. In case house No.5 is occupied by Rahu and Saturn, Venus in 11th house, Ketu in 8th and Jupiter in the 10th house there shall be illness initially to the partner and thereafter the son is likely to suffer. For this malady loaves of bread of flour of the weight of the son should be given to dogs for 25 to 48 days. If house 3 or 4 or 9 is afflicted the planet in house 5 shall give bad results. The planets in houses 6 or 10 will also give bad results without any regard whether they are friends or foes of the planet in house No. 5 Rahu and Ketu will influence the results according to their placement in the chart.

Sun is the lord of this house, Jupiter is the Karaka graha or the natural significator planet for the house.

House No. 6 is known as पाताल की दुनियाँ, रहम का खजाना और खुफिया मदद, that is, the hidden world, treasure house of mercy and providential help. House No. 6 is ruled by Mercury and hence the planet in house No. 6 is likely to afflict the results of house occupied by Mercury, Ketu or Venus. House No.6 is aspected by the planets in house No.2 and the house No.8 through house No.2. In such a case if Mercury or Rahu happens to be posited in house 6 there would be no bad effects of the malefics on the house because it is the house of exaltation for both of them. Ketu is the natural significator of the affairs of the house.

It has been said above the houses 2, 6 and 8 are mutually inter-connected with each other. While attempting any modification in any of the houses including the 6th house we have to keep in view all the three houses. If house No.6 is unoccupied there shall be no transfer of the afflictions of 8th and 2nd houses. There shall also be no aspect from 6th house to 12th house. The obvious result would be that the planets in 2nd and 12th houses will get extra strength. To avail of this opportunity if houses 2 and 3 are occupied by benefics it would always be helpful to awaken house No.6. This is possible by serving the maternal uncles (helping them) or serving the daughters of the daughter. Except Sun, Jupiter and Moon all the other planets in 6th house would be offering their on results. Mercury and Ketu will not offer good results till the age of the planet is in house 6 or 8. The question of the ages of planets will be dealt with at its proper place.

Although the planets in house No.6 are aspected by the planets in house No.2 yet the position would be reversed in the case of Saturn who will aspect house No.2 from 6th house.

House No.7 is known as गृहस्थी की चक्की or the family affairs, where the native has to struggle hard for fulfilling his material wants of bread, clothing and housing etc. It has been aptly described by Lal Kitab in the fallowing words.

आकाश जमीं दो पत्थर, सातवें रिज्क अकल की चक्की हो (The native gets ground between the earth and the sky for food). Here Akaash, Zameen, Rizque and Akal have been used metaphorically for Venus and Mercury because both these planets are the natural significators and Venus is also the lord of the house. The native sweats himself out in search of his food and clothing etc. Sun, Moon and Rahu offer the results according to the placement and position of Venus. Bad results due to the position of Venus cannot be improved or mitigated by remedies. In other words these results shall come to pass and the remedies will all go waste. Mercury, Saturn and Ketu shall give their results at various periods. If these results are bad we may try some remedial measures and they shall be set right or improved.

Normally the male planets affect the male relations and the female planets on affliction affect the female ones. In house 7 if the planets are more than two in number only the male relatives are affected. Sun, Mars and Jupiter are the male planets. Moon and Venus are females.

House No.8 deals with death and justice. Here justice means eye for eye and tooth for tooth. In other words the justice is on the basis of tit for tat.

It is the joint seat of Mars and Saturn. Both are the natural significators of the house. If Sun, Moon and Jupiter singly or jointly occupy this house the bad effects remain limited to house No.8 and its affairs. Saturn, Moon or Mars occupying this house singly give only good fruits. If, however, any two or all the three together join in this house they give bad results. Saturn will give death after death. Moon shall affect the health of the persons. Mars and Mercury occupying the house jointly give good results only if Saturn occupies house No.2. In such a case Mars shall be malefic or the negative Mars. House No.8 has its influence on house 6. If any of these houses is afflicted the results will be bad for both the houses. In such cases the planets in 12th house should also be judged. The planets may be friendly or inimical the planets in 12th house shall influence the results. Moon is the most powerful planet for the affairs of 8th house. Moon by strength of his placement and position can undo the ill of 12th house also. The cause of the malefic nature of 8th house will be house No.4 through house No.2. In other words the houses 2, 4 and 8 should be judged simultaneously. The planets in house 8, if inimical to planets in 2nd house and 11th will strike at the most vulnerable point.

House No.9 is known as आगाजे किस्मत the commencement of luck. Lucky period of the native shall start, good or bad, when the planet in this house becomes effective. The house is considered to be a great ocean. In case the house is inert, it can be activised through house No.2 if the other two houses namely the houses 3 and 5 are unoccupied. Any of the planets who has been dormant till he transits house No.9 and becomes active he will give results at his own age till his period is completed. Every planet has been assigned a particular period of age. By way of illustration, if Jupiter is in house 2 and transits the house in the progressed chart he will give results at the age of 16 and continue to do so till 16 years. Planets in house No.5 aspect the planets in house 9. If Sun or Moon occupy house 9 there will be no bad effects of even Rahu and Ketu. House No.9 is the seat of Jupiter.

House No. 10 is treated as the किस्मत की बुनियाद का मैदान, that is, the ground for the foundation of luck. The planet transiting the house, according to the progressed chart, becomes a doubtful planet. This is to say that nobody can be sure about the nature of results to be given by the planet. The planet in house 9 at the time of his transiting house 10 will give bad results even though the planets in house 6 and 5 are the friends. The nature of results would depend upon the nature of houses 8 and 2. The results will be bad if house 8 is afflicted and good if house 2 is in good shape. If house No. 10 is occupied by inimical planets their results shall be unpredictable. An idea of the nature of results can be formed from the position and placement of Moon. If Moon is benefic good results shall be obtained. In case house 10 is unoccupied the planets in house No.4 will not be able to give good results. Saturn is the natural significator of the house.

House No. 11 indicates all about the native's status and condition. Personal income and earnings of the native and his relation with the world at large can be judged from this house.

The results of Rahu and Ketu, if occupying 10th house, can be judged and they will be good normally if house No.3 is vacant. They will however, give bad results in house No.8.

Ketu in house No.11 would nullify the good effects of Moon and if Rahu occupies this house Jupiter's good results would be spoilt. Vice versa in each case would also be true.

Lal Kitab has given great importance to this house and planets in it. Even Rahu and Ketu give good results. If Rahu is a benefic the native shall not accept a single penny from his parents and whatever he gets will be lost to him due to one reason or the other; but all that he earns by the sweat of his own brow will be with him and give him pleasure.

House No.12 is the place of final rest according to the deeds or misdeeds of the native. House 10 reflects the physical valour etc., of the native but 12th deals with the character etc. If houses 2, 6 and 8 are occupied the native has good character. If houses 2 and 8 are occupied and there is no planet inimical to planet in 8th house the person shall command a keen intellect of very high order. If the life span is divided into 4 compartments we can judge how the native shall fare by the houses 1 to 3,4 to 6,7 to 9 and 10 to 12 in each part of his life respectively. Planet in No.11, its position and placement shall give a glimpse of worldly status of the native. This can be modified by the condition of house No.12. For improvement of the position of 12th house we look to house No. I and its planets. In other words, we can improve and get better results in house No. 12 if we can somehow improve the position of planets in lagna. If lagna is vacant we should go to house No.2 for improvement.

More about houses

In astrology we have a concept of the aspects of each planet irrespect of his placement in the chart. If it is assumed that Mars occupies the 7th house, we believe that he will aspect houses 10, 1 and 2 and may influence the results in those houses. This is not so in Lal Kitab. The first assumption there is that no planet aspects a house earlier than his own house. Mars in 7th house cannot aspect lagna or the 2nd house because they are the earlier houses than the 7th house. The birth chart can be divided in two parts for this purpose. First part shall consist of houses 1 to 6 and it is only in this part of the chart that the planets have aspects and that too to the houses subsequent to house occupied by the planet. There is only one exception to this general rule. Planet in house No.8 can and does aspect house No.2 of the chart.

The other important thing about aspects is that the particular house in which the planet is posited shall decide the house to be aspected by him. The planet in house 2 shall aspect the planet in house 6 and to none else by a 5th house aspect. Any planet in house 2 shall have this aspect. Normally the following aspects need be noted:

Planets in house No.	*aspect planets in house No.*
I	7
2	6
3	9, 11
4	10
5	9, 11
6	12
8	2

Houses are sleeping or inert if they are not occupied by any planet or not aspected by any planet. The sleeping houses can be awakened by propitiating various planets. Houses 9 and 11 can be a wakened by Jupiter. Moon can awaken houses 8, 4 and 2. For the houses 1 and 3 we need to propitiate Mars, and Mercury respectively. For houses 5, 6, 7, 10 and 12 the blessings of Sun, Rahu, Venus, Saturn and Ketu are necessary. In other words we can say that we can awaken or activate any house as per our requirements.

Yoga Drishti or Yoga aspects

Apart from the normal aspects there are Yoga aspects also. The houses or the planets in them look to the other house/planet for drawing power to fight against the cruel onslaughts of misfortunes and ill luck. These aspects of planets in certain houses get assistance of various types. The following table gives various Yoga drishtis.

House No,	*Aspects*	*Mutual help*	*General condition*	*Conflict*	*Basic help*	*Unpre- dictable*	*Sudden harm*
1	A	5	7	8	9	10	3
	B	9	7	6	5	4	
2	A	6	8	9	10	11	
	B	10	8	7	6	5	4
3	A	7	9	10	11	12	
	B	11	9	8	7	6	1
4	A	8	10	11	12	1	
	B	11	10	9	8	7	10
5	A	9	11	12	1	2	
	B	1	11	10	9	8	7
6	A	10	12	1	2	3	
	B	2	12	11	10	9	4
7	A	11	1	2	3	4	
	B	3	1	12	11	10	1
8	A	12	2	3	4	5	
	B	4	2	1	12	11	10
9	A	1	3	4	5	6	
	B	5	3	2	1	12	7
10	A	2	4	5	6	7	
	B	6	4	3	2	I	4
11	A	3	5	6	7	8	
	B	7	5	4	3	2	1
12	A	4	6	7	8	9	
	B	8	6	5	4	3	10

Notes :

(1) A : Indicates that the planet in the house shall help the planet in the column "Mutual help".

(2) B: Indicates that the planet in the house shall get help from the planet shown in the column of Mutual help.

(3) Basic help means that planets are very friendly. They may not mind losing their own identity in helping the other. They are just like milk and water. The latter loses its identity to increase 'the quantity of the former.'

(4) There is a column "Conflict". The planets in the particular house and the planets shown against the house "in conflict" will work as enemies whatever be their natural mutual relationship.

(5) The planets in column "Unpredictable" means that they may be good as well as bad in respect of the planets of the house against which they are written. If the planets give good results they will be doing double good and if bad they will do double bad.

(6) Sudden harm means that the planets irrespect of their mutual relationship will inflict injury or do harm so suddenly and quickly that the victim will not be able to judge the corner from where and how the misfortune overtook him.

In some cases the planets give their own results and some times they give the results of houses of their occupation. A list of such planets and houses is given below:

House	*Fruit of Planets*	*Fruit of Houses*
1.	Mars	Rahu
2.	Rahu and Ketu	–
3.	Saturn	Saturn (for wealth)
4.	Moon	Mars, Venus and Ketu
5.	Jupiter and Sun	–

6.	Mercury and Ketu	Sun, Mars, Jupiter, Saturn
7.	Venus	–
8.	Mars	–
9.	Jupiter	Saturn
10.	Saturn	Mercury and Ketu
11.	Jupiter and Saturn	–
12.	Rahu	Mercury

Remedies work when the planets give the results of house, as Rahu's results in 12th house are no amenable to remedies but those in the first house or lagna can be modified by suitable remedies. Those planets who give the results of the house are called Rasi Grahas.

Things pertaining to each house

House No.	*Direction*	*Wealth Income*	*Relations*	*Animals*	*Plants and trees*	*Property*
1.	East	Earned	Professional	Animals of upright horns & mammals	medicinal	self Purchased
2.	North-west	Savings	Beloved, in laws (Rahu in chart of males)	Pet Cows or oxen	Self planted (Kitchen garden)	House of in-laws
3.	South	Wealth of other relatives	Sisters, Brothers	Ferocious and wild animals	Stem of tree Fruit trees	of brothers, uncle etc.
4.	North East	Expenses	Mother and her parents	Aquatic animals milk animals, horse	juicy fruit trees	of maternal uncles & aunts
5.	Western wall	Wealth of children	Progeny, Ketu friend of progeny but enemy of maternal uncles	Animals of fir		of children
6.	North	Wealth of relatives	Behaviour of all relatives	Birds, dog, goat	Vegetables and flowers	of maternal uncles & aunts or of sister's children

House No.	*Direction*	*Wealth Income*	*Relations*	*Animals*	*Plants and trees*	*Property*
7.	South West	other's wealth for self	wife, daughters grand-daughter, sister (co-born)	Animals of downward horns, Birds, hens	Plumpy	of wife or the relatives of daughter
8.	Southern wall	Loss	Enemies, troubles, illness	scorpions, camels	Neither fruits nor flowers	graveyard
9.	open place in the centre of house	Savings of elders	Elders	Frogs, buffalo cows, dogs water animals	Roots and those things that remain underground	Ancestral Property
10.	West	Father's property	father's comforts	Serpent, and animals having tails	Thorny trees	Father's old and own constructed house more than 3 years
11.	Western wall	Income	Parental wealth at birth	Serpent with two mouths	Shady trees (not thorny)	Purchased Property
12.	South East	Pleasures of bed and relations of wife or husband		cats, bats, fish		Property of neighbours

3

The Planets

Lal Kitab deals with nine oldest known planets, namely Sun, Moon, Mars, Jupiter, Venus, Mercury, Saturn, Rahu and Ketu. Though the last two are the nodes yet they are also treated like the planets.

There are many types of classifications of these planets. Some of them are just the same as we have in regular astrology. The planets are classified as males and females. Sun, Mars, and Jupiter are the male planets. Moon and Venus are females. Saturn and Mercury are the eunuchs. Rahu and Ketu are just the associates of Saturn. They have not been assigned any sex.

The rasis ruled by these planets are also the same. Sun rules over Leo, Moon over Cancer, Mars over Aries and Scorpio, Mercury over Gemini and Virgo, Jupiter over Sagittarius and Pisces, Venus over Taurus and Libra, and Saturn over Capricorn and Aquarius. As regards the nodes, Rahu shares his lordship of Pisces with Jupiter and Ketu is the joint lord of Virgo with Mercury.

As regards houses of exaltations and debilitations of these planets they are also the same as in regular astrology. Sun gets exalted in Aries, Moon in Taurus, Jupiter in Cancer, Mercury and Rahu in Virgo, Saturn in Libra, Ketu in Sagittarius, Mars in Capricorn and Venus and Ketu in Pisces. Rahu gets exalted in Gemini also. The houses of debilitation of each planet are the houses 180 degrees apart from their houses of exaltation. In birth charts rasis are identical with houses.

There is similarity between traditional astrology and Lal Kitab upto this place. One peculiarity of Lal Kitab is that the rasis are not taken into account. The numbers of Rasis which are taken to be identical with house numbers, are only important.

Pakka Ghar of Planets

Pakka Ghar is nothing but the concept of natural significators of houses. Sun's Pakka Ghar is lagna. The other planets' Pakka Ghars are as under:

Sun	Lagna
Moon	4th house
Mars	3rd & 8th houses
Mercury	7th house
Jupiter	2nd, 5th, 9th and 11th houses
Venus	7th house
Saturn	8th and 10th houses

Friends and Foes of Planets

Each planet has his friends as well as his enemies just as we human beings do. The list is as under—

Planet	*Friends*	*Enemies*
Sun	Jupiter, Mars, Moon	Venus, Saturn, Rahu & Ketu
Moon	Sun, Mercury	Ketu, Rahu
Mars	Sun, Moon, Jupiter	Mercury, Ketu
Mercury	Sun, Venus, Rahu	Moon
Jupiter	Sun, Moon, Mars	Venus Mercury
Venus	Saturn, Mercury, Ketu	Sun, Moon, Rahu
Saturn	Mercury, Venus, Rahu	Sun, Moon, Mars
Rahu	Mercury, Ketu, Saturn	Sun Venus Mars
Ketu	Venus, Rahu	Moon, Mars

Apart from the friendship or enemity of planets there is also a concept of equivalent planets. The planets so grouped are supposed to be equal in strength. The list of such planets is as under:

Planets individually equal to	*Planets*
Mercury*	Sun
Venus, Saturn, Jupiter and Mars	Moon
Venus, Saturn, and Rahu*	Mars
Saturn, Ketu, Mars and Jupiter	Mercury
Rahu, Ketu and Saturn	Jupiter
Mars and Jupiter	Venus
Ketu and Jupiter	Saturn
Jupiter and Moon	Rahu
Jupiter, Saturn, Mercury and Sun	Ketu

*When Mercury and Sun or Rahu and Mars are posited in one sign together Mercury or Rahu would always be quiet.

Moon and Sun when posited in any sign with Rahu and Ketu respectively will be less powerful.

Artificial planets

Lal Kitab has a concept that a group of two planets are equivalent to the planet noted against each. The list is as under:

group or Planets	
Mercury and Venus together represent	Sun
Sun and Jupiter together represent	Moon
Sun and Mercury together represent	Positive Mars
Sun and Saturn together represent	Negative Mars
Jupiter and Rahu together represent	Mercury
Sun and Venus together represent	Jupiter
Rahu Ketu together represent	Venus
Jupiter & Venus together represent	Saturn (like Ketu)

Mars and Mercury together represent	Saturn (like Ketu)
Mars and Saturn together represent	Rahu exalted
Sun and Saturn together represent	Rahu Debilitated
Venus and Saturn together represent	Ketu exalted
Moon and Saturn together represent	Ketu debilitated

In the above classification it appears that the author of Lal Kitab has made detailed study of the nature of planets, particularly of Rahu, Ketu and Saturn. The list of artificial planets is also useful in finding out remedies.

Sin and Sinful planets

Often there is a reference of Paap (Sin) and Paapi (Sinful) planets in Lal Kitab. From Paap or Sin is meant Rahu and Ketu from Paapi grahas the reference is to three planets namely Rahu, Ketu and Saturn.

Kayam Graha or Established Planet

The planet which can give his results freely and without hindrance is called an established planet. In other words no enemy planet should occupy his houses of lordship, exaltation, debility and of his signification. He should also not be a Saathi planet or comrade and he should have no aspect of any planet.

Dharmi Grahas or Righteous Planets

Saturn, Rahu and Ketu are known as Paapi planets but they also sometimes become the Dharmi or righteous planets. Rahu and Ketu become righteous in the 4th house or anywhere in the chart with Moon. Similarly Saturn becomes righteous when posited in the 11th house or anywhere in the chart with Jupiter.

By becoming righteous they do not give good results or become benefics. They shall not simply afflict the house or the planet. They become neutral. They on their part will not promote or cause any bad effects. They shall be least bothered if some other planet does it. In giving their results they will not be bad.

Muqabla ke Graha or Matching planets

Each planet has his own friends who behave in a friendly way. Sometimes one of such planets may occupy the house of lordship or the Pakka Ghar of his friendly planet and that planet does not occupy any such house of the former. In such a case the two planets, although friends, may not remain true friends. The behaviour of the former will be suspected. He may at times spoil the results of his friendly planet. This planet shall be known as a matching planet. Sun and Mars are friends. If Mars occupies the lagna and Sun does not occupy such house of Mars. Mars' behaviour under such circumstances may or may not be friendly to Sun. Mars would be called a matching planet to Sun. Both can harm each other.

Planetary results and remedial measures

When a particular planet starts giving bad or undesirable results we start indulging in various remedial measures. These measures in some cases may be helpful but they cannot be helpful in all the cases. When the planet has to give his own results that is the results he has to give under the Providential scheme of things, there shall be no respite from them. In order to identify the cases where the remedial measures shall work we have to study the position of the planet and his placement. At some places he is the rasi graha.

Every planet has his houses of lordship, exaltation, debilitation or Pakka ghar. If a planet is posited in anyone of such houses he will give his own results. There shall be no escape from them. No remedies shall work even to tone down the effects much less to change them. This power to have any modifications etc. is not given to any normal human being. This is not to say that the results can never be modified or improved upon. For such a miracle we need some godman or very enlightened soul but even such enlightened soul has to pay the price by submitting himself to the torture. In other words even such persons can only change the course of floods and not avoid them. Emperor Babar did save the life of Humayun but he paid the price for it by his own life.

The toll, life for life, was taken to meet the ends of justice. Even this power is not granted to average mortals.

The planet is amenable to remedies like cajoling, flattering or keeping him in good humour by suitable measures only if he does not occupy any of his own houses. Remedies can and do help in such cases.

Blind Planets

If the planets in house 10 are in debility or malefics or inimical to each other or are afflicted they become blind planets. Their behaviour shall be unpredictable. Nothing can be taken for granted.

Comrade Planets

Sometimes Planets exchange their rasis. They may be houses of exaltation, debilitation or Pakka Ghar. When two planets occupy each other's identical houses both the planets become comrades or Saathis even though they are inimical to each other. Sun is an enemy of Saturn. The Pakka ghar of Sun is the 5th house and that of Saturn is the 10th house. If Sun occupies the 10th house and Saturn the 5th the two shall be comrades.

If the friendly planets occupy the two adjacent houses they shall also be comrades. If the planets occupying adjacent houses are inimical to each other they shall not be comrades.

The Sacrificial goats of planets

Often the planets quarrel if they are inimical. One tries to spoil the results of the other. They afflict each other. In such afflictions or quarrels weaker planet passes his liability to some other planet and thus gets the other plane's results spoiled. According to Lal Kitab the sacrificial planets are as under:

Saturn's affliction

When there is an affliction to Saturn the consequences shall be passed on Venus, that is, the trouble shall come to the wife of the native.

Mercury'S affliction

Mercury in his case of affliction shall pass on the trouble to Venus or to say the same thing otherwise, Venus will take the misfortunes of Mercury over himself and thus the victim would be the wife of the native.

Mars' affliction

The affliction of Mars is passed on to Ketu. The son of the native is likely to suffer. If Sun is in the 6th house and Mars in the 10th house the son of the native will suffer. Son here may mean son as well as the nephew of the native.

Venus' affliction

If Venus is afflicted the mother of the native may be the victim because Venus passes on his troubles to Moon. If Moon and Venus become the matching planets the mother of the native may become blind.

Jupiter's affliction

Jupiter passes on the trouble to Ketu like Mars. If Jupiter occupies the 5th house the period of Jupiter and Ketu shall be bad for maternal uncle of the native.

Sun also does the same. The maternal uncle will suffer from the bad results. Similarly Moon's bad results are passed on to Jupiter/Mars/Sun. Rahu and Ketu do not do any such mischief. They face the consequences themselves.

All this indirectly means that bad results of the planets are apparent on the condition of the persons (relatives) or the relevant profession etc. of the planet who is offering the bad results.

Deceptive Planets

Sometimes the planets in themselves do not indicate whether they would be giving good results or bad results. If they give good results they will do it with double speed. If they are to offer bad results the same would be done with double speed. Such position of planets arises mostly when the planets transit house No.10. Following principles on which planets work are given in the Lal Kitab.

The planet transiting house No.10 in the annual progressed chart shall be the deceptive planet in the sense of offering his results. It is not that the planet shall not give results but that the nature of its results, good or bad, cannot be predicted precisely. If the planet in 8th house is giving bad results the planet in house 10 shall give bad results. If house No.2 has benefic planets the results of the planet in 10th house shall be good. In case the 2nd house is good and the 8th bad, the results given by the planet in the 10th house would be mixed, that is, good as well as bad. The good results will be offered earlier and the bad ones later on.

The results of the planet in 10th house would depend upon the houses No.3, 5 and 9. If the houses 2 and 8 are unoccupied. In case houses 3, 5 and 9 are also vacant the position of Saturn should be examined. The results would be in accordance with his position and placement.

If the house No.10 is occupied by the planets who are mutually quarrelling or are mutually inimical, they will be called the blind planets, that is, nothing much can be said about them in advance. In such a case the results would depend upon the position of Moon. If Moon is in a good position the results shall be good, and if bad, the results would be bad.

If house No.10 is unoccupied no results can be expected from the planets in 4th house. To obtain good results from house. No.4 in such a case the native should indulge in the service of his parents and grand parents etc. Alternatively ten blind persons should be given food.

Rahu, Ketu and Mercury in house No.10 singly or jointly will always be deceptive in their behaviour. They will depend upon their results on the condition etc. of Saturn.

Aspects of planets (general)

In normal conditions aspect means the normal course in which the planets affect each other. There are no mutual aspects of planets in Lal Kitab.

The planets in house No.1 aspect the planets in house No.7; but the latter does not aspect the former. Aspect here further means that the aspecting planet can mix up his poison or *amrit* in the results of the aspected planets. The normal aspects are as under:

Planets in house No.	*aspect planets in House No.*
1	7
2	6
3	9 and 11
4	10
5	9
6	12
8	2

Yoga Drishti of Planets for help

The above table indicates the aspects where one planet can affect the results of other planets by aspect. Here is the table showing the aspects of planets for mutual help.

1.	Planets in house No. 1	seek help from planets in No.5
2.	Planets in house No.2	seek help from planets in No.6
3.	Planets in house No.3	seek help from planets in No.7
4.	Planets in house No.4	seek help from planets in No.8
5.	Planets in house No.5	seek help from planets in No.9
6.	Planets in house No.6	seek help from planets in No.10
7.	Planets in house No.7	seek help from planets in No.11
8.	Planets in house No.8	seek help from planets in No.12

9.	Planets in house No. 9	seek help from planets in No.1
10.	Planets in house No. 10	seek help from planets in No.2
11.	Planets in house No. 11	seek help from planets in No.3
12.	Planets in house No. 12	seek help from planets in No.4

Here the assistance shall be available to the planets irrespect of mutual disposition of the planets to each other.

Affliction of planets

Even the most friendly planets behave like die-hard foes and shake the stricken planets to their roots.

Planets in house No. 1	give a jolt to planets in house 8
Planets in house No. 2	give a jolt to planets in house 9
Planets in house No. 3	give a jolt to planets in house 10
Planets in house No. 4	give a jolt to planets in house 11
Planets in house No. 5	give a jolt to planets in house 12
Planets in house No. 6	give a jolt to planets in house 1
Planets in house No. 7	give a jolt to planets in house 2
Planets in house No. 8	give a jolt to planets in house 3
Planets in house No. 9	give a jolt to planets in house 4
Planets in house No. 10	give a jolt to planets in house 5
Planets in house No. 11	give a jolt to planets in house 6
Planets in house No. 12	give a jolt to planets in house 7

Articles pertaining to combination of planets

Planets	*alticlcs*
Jupiter Ketu	yellow lemon
Jupiter Moon	Banyan tree
Sun Moon	Milk of banyan tree; Leechi (लीची), Horse
Sun Venus	Red stone, Burnt clay, glass of kansa metal
Sun Mercury	Red alum, white glass

Moon Mercury	Mother and daughter, Sand in river water
Moon Saturn	Black ink, well, Tortoise, fermented milk vehicles, Poisonous milk
Venus Mars	*Tandoor* of *clay*. Geru (गेरू)
Venus Mercury	Artificial Sun, Weighing scale, Flour mill
Venus Saturn	Black peeper and ghee
Mars (negative) and Mercury	Magnifying glass, flower of *anar* (अनार), Bright red clothes of a girl
Mars (Positive) and Mercury	Bright red clothes worn by girls in marriage.
Mars Saturn	Coconut. Dates.
Mercury Saturn	Mango tree

Things pertaining to Planets

Planets	*Deity*	*Vocation*	*Metals/ Precious stones*	*Body Parts*	*On the face*	*Animals*	*Colour of Planet*	*Remedies*	*Other things of Remedies*
Sun	Lord Vishnu	Kshatri Rajput	Copper Ruby	Whole body	Right Portion	Monkey Hilly Cow	wheatish	Harivamsa Purana	Wheat, Red Copper
Moon	Lord Shiva	Concerning Water and liquid	Silver, Pearl (milky white)	Heart	Left Portion	Horse Mare	Milky white	Worship of Personal god/ goddess	Rice Milk Silver
Mars (Positive)	Lord Hanuman	Warrior	Not bright but red precious stone	Liver	upper lip	Tiger	Red	Gayatri Paath	Masoor Dal (Red)
Mars (Negative)	ghosbts	Tyrant	Bright red stone	Liver	Lower lip	Camel Deer	-do-	-do-	-do-
Mercury	Goddess Durga	Trader Broker	Diamond Emerald	Brain skull, Tongue, Teeth, Nerves	Tip of Nose	Goat Sheep Bat	Green	Durga Paath	Moong (not the pulse)
Jupiter	Lord Brahma (Creator)	Concerning gold	Gold Topaz	Neck	Nose	Lion, Lioness	Yellow Pale	Hari Poojan	Pulse (gram) Gold

Planet	*Deity*	*Vocation*	*Metals/ Precious stones*	*Body Parts*	*On the face*	*Animals*	*Colour of Planet*	*Remedies*	*Other things of Remedies*
Venus	Goddess Lakshmi	Goldsmith Trader agriculturist landlord	Clay, Pearl of Curd White Colour	Checks	Cheeks	Cow, ox	Like Curd	Feeding the persons	Butter curd Camphor Pearl (white)
Saturn	Lord Bhairon	Blacksmith Cobbler	Iron, Steel	Vision (eyes)	Hair, eyebrows	Buffalo	Black	Worship of king	Urad (not broken) BlackSmith
Rahu	Goddess Saraswati	Sweeper or doing lower job like peon	Sapphire Gomed	Mental vibrations Head	Chin	Elephant wild rat	Blue	Kanya daan (arranging marriage of girls and spending on them)	Mustard Sapphire
Ketu	Lord Ganesha	Free from social or religious customs	Vaidurya	Whole body except head	Ear, feet Spine, Knees ankles	Dog, Donkey, Pig, Lizard	Multicoloured (at least two colours)	Giving Cow (who has not been pregnant even once) in charity	Til

4

More about planets

After giving the various classifications of the planets it is necessary to say how the Lal Kitab takes the planets themselves. In astrology we take Sun as the ruler of the universe and ascribe all the good qualities to him. In cases of affliction the same good qualities get perverted. The quality of a good ruler is his benevolence. When he is afflicted this benevolence turns into tyranny. A few words about each of the nine planets of Lal Kitab would be necessary.

JUPITER

Sun is, no doubt, the ruler of the solar system according to Lal Kitab but more importance is given to Jupiter. The reasons given for this are simple. The two nodes Rahu and Ketu are described as the Dragon's head and Dragon's tail. In other words these two planets are the two extremes of the human body. The parts lying in between the two extremes, that is, head and tail or head and feet are governed by the other planets. Jupiter rules neck portion of the body which joins the two extremes. Bringing together the two extremes is a praise-worthy feet of Jupiter and naturally enough Jupiter should be given more importance than any other planet. Even otherwise also, Jupiter is considered the preceptor of gods. Sun is included in that list. Preceptor does not rule but does command respect from the highest and the lowest including the ruler.

Jupiter is known as the Akaash or the space where the air moves about freely. He goes about the two worlds the Iha-loka and Para-loka, that is, the material and spiritual worlds. He rules the 9th and 12th signs of natural zodiac and houses 5 and 9 of the birth chart. Twelfth sign of the zodiac or 12th house of the chart is supposed to be the joint seat of Jupiter and Rahu. When the former is confronted in the 12th house with Rahu the latter gets precedence. Jupiter simply yields to Rahu. He becomes the man of this world.

Jupiter like other planets has his friends and foes. The list of friends and foes appears elsewhere but even his foes give regard to him in certain position. Mercury is the enemy of Jupiter but when Mercury occupies houses 2, 5, 9 or 11 the results given by Mercury are those of Jupiter. In these houses Mercury will not go against Venus, Sun, Jupiter and Saturn. In other words every thing depends upon the placement of the planet. However, Jupiter becoming weak, will follow Mercury's nature and will not give good results in any respects if connected with Mercury, Venus, Saturn and Rahu or Ketu.

Out of 35 years cycle of planets Jupiter has 6 years span. He is the planet for Rashi-phal in houses 6 and 7 of the chart. His ill effects can be nullified by suitable remedial measures.

Lord Brahma is his deity, brass and Topaz the metal and gem and religious places are his places. Goldsmith is his profession. He represents father, grandfather, priests, wandering priests, and family priests. Peepal tree is governed by him. Saffron, Haldi, pulses and gram are the articles of Jupiter.

By suitable propitiation of Jupiter we can awaken the vacant 9th and 11th houses.

GENERAL REMEDIES

JUPITER

For bad results when Jupiter is

In lagna

1. The remedies as given in Rin Pitri.
2. Do not accept charity or help from any body. Have faith on your own luck.

In 2nd house

1. Filling the pit on the road in front of the house.
2. Tilak of Kesar or Haldi.

In 3rd house

Durga Poojan or giving sweets to the girls and obtain their blessings

In 4th house

1. Have a red mark on the underwear used below the shirt.
2. Service of elders.
3. Do not take bath in front of anybody. Do not show your bare body (the parts normally remaining under the clothes) to any body.
4. Going to places of worship and doing Pooja.
5. Obtain the blessings of your family priest.
6. Plant a Peepal Tree or water a Peepal tree.

In 5th house

1. Do not accept alms or any thing, even the Prasad from temples etc.
2. Do not accept any thing free of cost.
3. Have a choti on head.
4. Service of Sadhus and cleaning the places of worship.

In 6th house

1. Articles concerning Jupiter be given to temples.
2. Business with own children or on their advice.
3. Feeding the cocks or keeping them as pets.
4. Clothes to the priest of the temple.

In 7th house

1. Do not keep Mala, Tulsi plant, or the deity in the house. Photo on the walls are allowed.
2. Gold or gold ornaments to be kept tied in yellow cloth.
3. Be away from the Sadhu wearing yellow clothes.

In 8th house

1. Wear gold ornaments.
2. Giving ghee, curd, potatoes, and camphor to places of worship.
3. Beggar should not go disappointed.

In 9th house

1. Holy dip in Ganges and drinking Ganges water.
2. Visiting holy places and helping others visiting holy places.
3. Speak the truth, be religious.

In 10th house

1. Do not do good to any body.
2. No service to the preceptor or religious persons or the Peepal tree.
3. Do not wear yellow clothes or gold.
4. Cleaning the nose before starting the work.
5. Throw copper coin in the running water daily for 43 days.

In the 11th house

1. Keep a yellow hanky.

2. Use the bed and clothes which *father* has used.
3. Watering the Peepal tree.

In the 12th house

1. Do not be a false witness.
2. Do not cheat any body.
3. Service of preceptor, Sadhu or Peepal tree.

General Remedies for all ills

1. Fasting on Thursdays.
2. Worshipping Lord Hari or watering Peepal tree.
3. Wearing topaz or tying a haldi piece in a yellow thread round the right arm.
4. Tilak of Haldi or Kesar to a silver vessel.
5. Service of Brahman, family priest or a sadhu.
6. Reciting Garuda Purana.
7. Planting the yellow flower-plants.
8. If Jupiter is debilitated, give in charity the commodities pertaining to Jupiter.

SUN

Sun gives us heat, light and energy. He is thus the preserver of life. His deity as such is Lord Vishnu. Sun always seems to be moving and that too in one direction; but no body knows his destination. The only thing we know about him is that he does not change his course and also does not retrace his steps.

Sun is like a king who listens to every body and sees everything but nobody knows what he will do next. Jupiter gets precedence over him. Sun may be taken as the second ruler. He represents the soul and the lordship of world. He is a benevolent ruler of this world. He is pious and observing penance. He does not believe in any particular religion but he is the most religious ruler. He knows what is right and what is wrong and gives judgement on that basis. In the 7th house, as in the 7th rasi of the Zodiac he is considered debilitated but that he never becomes. He, however, becomes malefic and benefic as per his placement in any particular chart. The native who has his Sun in lagna may achieve great heights but will not be able to enjoy the fruits of his attainments. His ego comes in the way. His forth-right expression is his handicap. If he can regulate or keep under proper control his ego he will be a lucky man.

Sun will give very good results if Ketu occupies house 1 or 6. Sun's occupation of the house will be immaterial. If Sun aspects Mercury everything concerning ladies in the house will be good. Similarly if Mercury aspects Sun, the results of Mercury will be good. If Saturn aspects Sun the influence of Sun may get a set back but things concerning Venus will get a boost. Saturn will give some set back to Sun but this will not affect the earnings of the native or his well being. There may be some physical ailments. If Sun occupies houses earlier to Saturn or aspects him the ladies in the house will suffer severe strokes of misfortune.

If Sun gets the help of Moon, Mars or Jupiter and the native is in the habit of taking no or very little salt the native shall rise much above his present-status.

In case house 5 has no planet in it Sun should be propitiated. It can be activised. In the 35 year cycle of planets Sun has a span of 2 years. In the chart Sun in houses 6 and 7 will be planet of rasi and if it starts giving bad results the same would be amenable to the remedies.

Gold and copper are the metals and ruby is the precious stone of Sun. The body parts governed by him are native's body in general and his right eye and bones in particular. Sun has domain over service or works concerning the government, grey beer, grey mangoes, white ant, fruit trees, white salt, gur (jaggery), wheat, bajra, monkey and the only son.

Remedies

In lagna

1. Maintain good moral character.
2. Construct a dark room on the left hand side of the house in the end.

In the 2nd house

1. Instal a hand pump in the ancestral house.
2. Do not take any thing free. Do not take in charity the things pertaining to Moon like rice, silver or milk etc.
3. Maintain good moral character.
4. Giving coconuts, oil or almonds to temple.

In 3rd house

1. Maintain good moral character.
2. Getting blessings of mother/grandmother.

In 4th house

1. Feed the blind.
2. Never use wine. No eating or hunting fish.
3. Copper coin tied in a Khaki thread should be used around the neck.

In 5th house.

1. Do not tell a lie and have no ill will against any body.
2. Promises should be honoured.
3. Follow the old traditions and customs.
4. Monkeys of red face should be fed with jaggery (gur).
5. Service of three classical dogs.

   (Brother at sister's house, Son-in-law at father-in-law's house and the son of the daughter at the house of maternal uncles.)

In 6th house

1. Feeding monkeys with wheat and jaggery.
2. White ants to be given seven cereals. This may be kept in the field or park under trees on the ground.
3. Keeping silver or river water with him.
4. Washing the feet of mother and grand-mother.
5. Bury under ground copper piece (square in shape).

In 7th house

1. Use milk to extinguish the fire after cooking in the night and that *chulha* should not be used again before the following dawn.
2. Bury Copper pieces as above.
3. Feeding the black cow or the cow without horns.
4. Start the work after eating some sweets and drinking water.
5. After cooking, put some piece of bread etc in the burning fire of *chulha*.

In 8th house

1. The house should not have the main entrance from the south.
2. Keep a white cow.
3. Maintain good moral character.
4. Do not live with in-laws.
5. Service of *elder* brother and cow.

In 9th house

1. Use brass vessels.
2. Do not accept alms of milk, rice or silver.
3. Never be very angry or too tolerant. Be normal.

In 10th house

1. Wear white cap or turban.

2. Instal a hand pump in the ancestral house.
3. Service of grey buffalo.

In 11th house

1. Do not drink wine or eat fish. Do not do fishing.
2. Never tell a lie.
3. Purchasing a goat form .butcher and setting it free, that is, allowing it one life more.

In the 12th house

1. Never work like a mechanic.
2. There should be a court yard in the house.

General Remedies

1. Fast on Sunday.
2. Reciting or listening to Harivansha Purana
3. Wheat, jaggery and copper etc. to be given in charity.
4. Maintaining good moral character.
5. Wearing Ruby or in place of Ruby copper can be used.
6. Throwing copper coin in the flowing water.
7. Keep main entrance from east.
8. Keeping away from black marketing and black marketeers.
9. Do not give in alms the article pertaining to Sun if Sun is exalted.
10. Service of Government officials.

MOON

Moon is the mother. Mother needs the heat of Sun for the welfare of her child. Excessive or little heat are both harmful and against the interest of the child. It is for this reason that Moon goes round the Sun and does not stay on the way. It also does not retrace its steps. While we are not sure of the destination of Sun we are pretty sure of the destination of

Moon. Her destination is the well being of the child. As the mother, Moon governs the longevity and also the heart of the native because heart beat is the sign of life. In the natural zodiac Moon rules over the 4th sign and in the chart the 4th house comes under her sway.

Moon does not give good effects when Jupiter and Ketu occupy earlier and latter houses respectively from Moon provided Mercury is a malefic. Even the sleeping Moon will give good results if Mercury is favourable. If Venus aspects Moon the native will face opposition from females, but if it is the other way round the native may become a man of supernatural powers. Any planet occupying the 4th house alone will give good results. If the house is unoccupied the lord of the house, Moon shall give good results in respect of the house. By touching the feet of his elders and obtaining their blessings the native can get still better fruits. If Moon occupies house earlier than Mercury the former shall influence the effects of the later. There may be no apparent material gains but providential help in times of need will always be forthcoming. If, however, Mercury and Moon happen to be in the house 4 or 7 together they will never give good results.

If Moon aspects Saturn there will be no bad effects on Moon. If the position is otherwise the results of Moon shall be affected adversely. There will be effect of Saturn on Moon. The native governed by Saturn will not he benefitted in the trade or business concerning Venus. If Moon aspects Rahu, Ketu or Saturn the bad effects shall pass on to the relatives concerning the planet. Moon is generally not a benefic when Sun and Mars are together in a sign or a house. If Moon aspects Jupiter and houses 2, 5, 9 and 12 are Occupied by Mercury, Venus, Rahu and Saturn respectively Moon will not give good results.

If houses 2, 4 or 8 are vacant or inert, Moon has to be propitiated. In the 35 years cycle of the planets Moon's span is one year. Lord Shiva is his deity. Silver, rice, mill water (wells, ponds etc.) and pearl of white colour are the articles of Moon and heart and the left eye are the parts of body governed by her. Horse and rabit are the animals and mother, mother's sister and mother and grand mother are the relatives coming under her domain.

Remedies for ills in various houses

In lagna

1. Drop a copper coin in the river when crossing it with the children.
2. Obtain blessings of mother and keep rice and silver given by her on person.
3. Copper nails in the feet of bed.
4. Either keep a cow or a maid servant in the 24th year of age.
5. Do not get married before the age of 28 years.
6. Do not construct a house before the age of 24 years.
7. Drink water or milk in silver vessel.

In the 2nd house

1. Silver brick should be buried in the foundation of the house.
2. As per No.2 in lagna.

In the 3rd house

1. Rice, silver and milk should be given in alms on the birthday of the daughter and wheat, copper and jaggery on the birth day of the son.
2. Durga Puja.
3. Kanya Daan.

In the 4th house

1. No trade or business in dairy products like milk, butter, cheese etc.
2. Business in cloth in partnership with mother or under her advice is useful.

In the 5th house

1. Sometimes do religious acts.
2. Sometimes go to hilly places.

In the 6th house

1. Do not give out your secrets to any body.
2. Keep rabits as pets.
3. No arrangements where general public may take free water.

In the 7th house

1. Maintain good moral character.
2. Do not get married in the 24th or 25th year.

In the 8th house

1. Giving alms in the name of dead elders.
2. Installing a hand pump in the hospital or in the crematoriums.
3. Giving articles of Jupiter, Sun or Mars in temples and religious places.

In the 9th house

1. Visiting the places of worship.
2. Maintain good conduct.

In the 10th house

1. If a doctor, do not give free medicines.
2. Maintain good moral character.
3. Do not take milk at night.

In the 11th house

1. Native's mother should not see her grandson till 43 days of his birth.
2. Milk for the temple of Bhairon.
3. Children under the age of nine years should be fed with 121 (11 x 11) Pedas.

In the 12th house

1. In 16 litres of rain water drop 4 silver ingots and keep them under the roof of the house.

General remedies

1. Keep fast on Monday.
2. Worship Lord Shiva or go on pilgrimage to Amarnath.
3. Milk, rice or silver to be given in alms.
4. Wear a white milky pearl or alternatively silver can be substituted.
5. Blessings of mother (grand mother, mother-in-law, mother's mother, mother's sister).
6. Silver nails in the feet of the bed.
7. Silver or rice to be dropped in the Crematorium.
8. Taking bath in the Ganges or running water.
9. Water tank over head should be cleaned in 3 to 6 months.
10. No water pump or well under the roof.
11. Giving things pertaining to Moon in charity if Moon is in debility but not when she is in exaltation.

VENUS

Venus is considered as the preceptor of demons who love sex and physical comforts. They are not concerned with any religion or philosophy. Venus stands for them. Venus alone occupying any house is never bad.

If Mercury occupied houses 1, 2 or 3 from Venus the results individually and jointly will be good. Ketu will also give good results. If the case is otherwise Rahu will be poisoning their effects. If Venus and Mercury appear in houses *2-8,3-9,6-12* and 8-2 respectively the results of the two houses occupied by them will be bad but this is not possible because they are never so far away from each other. If, however, Mercury is in 6th house and Venus in the 12th (both are exalted) they will give good results. When Rahu aspects Venus or vice versa the good results of Venus will be nullified. If in the birth chart, Venus will be affected whenever Venus in the progressed chart is posited in malefic houses.

Her deity is goddess Lakshmi. Diamond is the precious stone and silver is the metal. Wife and the lady lover are the persons governed by Venus. Camphor, ghee, curd, cotton and the aromatic shrubs or any vocation concerning them come within the domain of Venus. Face is the part of the body governed by her. Venus activises the 7th house and is the planet of Rashiphal in the 4th house. Her span is 3 years in the 35 year cycle of planets.

Remedies for the Ills of Venus

In the Lagna

1. Some portion of food served to cow, dog and the bird.
2. Accepting pure silver from in-laws.
3. Using cow urine.
4. Giving barley and mustard in alms. 5. The wife should wear gold on head. 6. Having firm faith in God.

In the 2nd house

1. Keeping quadrupeds as business.
2. Potatoes, curd and butter in charity.

In the 3rd house

1. Using the articles of Mars.
2. Stop dancing and music in the house.

In the 4th house

1. Marrying his own wife twice.
2. Maintaining good conduct.

In 5th house

1. Maintain good moral character.
2. Serve the cows.
3. No love marriage or marriage against the wishes of parents.

4. Private parts should be washed with milk by the native and his wife.

In the 6th house

1. Due regard to be given to all females.
2. The women folk should never be bare foot on the ground, not even in kitchen or bath room.

In the 7th house

1. White cow should not be fed or served.
2. Bronze vessels should be taken as gifts in dowry.

In the 8th house

1. The native should not accept Daan (taking free things as charity or in the name of God etc).
2. Bowing head in the temples and places of worship.
3. Copper coin or some flower to be thrown in the gutter/ dirty nalla.

In the 9th house

1. In the foundation of the house silver and honey should be buried.
2. Silver bangles to be worn after having some red colours on them.
3. Bury a silver piece under a Neem tree.

In the 10th house

1. Western wall of the house should be of mud (Kachhi)
2. No wine or non-vegetarianism and no fishing also.

In the 11th house

1. Remedies of Mercury will be useful.
2. Oil to be given on Saturdays.

In the 12th house

1. Giving cow in charity.
2. Blue flowers to be buried by the wife.
3. Any charity by wife.
4. Pure ghee lamp.

General Remedies

1. Fast on Friday.
2. Desi ghee, curd, camphor etc. to be given to places of worship.
3. Wear diamond or pearl.
4. Perfuming the clothes and using cream and face powder etc.
5. Clothes should be clean and ironed.
6. Worn out clothes or burnt clothes should never be worn.

MARS

Mars has been classified as Mars positive and Mars negative. The main peculiarity of Mars is that he cannot be a fence-sitter or a middle path goer. He should be on the extreme, this way or that way. The couplet describes him Well.

"दो रंग अच्छी न, एक रंग हो जा। सरासर तू हो मोम या संग हो जा। In other words, dualism is not good. Either become soft like wax or hard like a stone.

Mars would be Mars positive if Sun and Mercury are in a sign together. He becomes negative Mars if Saturn and Sun are in the same sign. In fact Mars is neither a natural malefic nor a natural benefic. He becomes this or that according to the circumstances of each case.

Mars is benefic

1. If Saturn with Rahu or Ketu occupies a house together;
2. If two enemies like Mercury and Ketu occupy a house jointly.

3. If Moon and Venus, together or singly occupy any of the houses 3, 4 or 8. Even if Mars is with one or the other or with both he will be a benefic.
4. If Moon is wasting himself in any of the houses 1, 4, 7, or, 10;
5. If Sun is posited in 6th house;
6. If Sun, Moon or Jupiter is in houses 3, 4, 7, 8 and 9 . If friends of Mars are helping him.

   Sun does not help Mars if :

   (a) Sun is in houses 5 or 9 with Ketu.

   (b) Sun is in houses 6 or 12 with Rahu.

   (c) Sun is in house 7 with Venus.

   (d) Sun is in house 10 with Saturn.

   (e) Sun is in house 12 with Mercury.

   (f) Sun is in houses 1 or 8 without Mars.

Sun, Moon or Jupiter do not help Mars if they are not occupying houses 3, 4 or 8. Mars becomes a malefic if he occupies any of these houses singly and the other two houses occupied by Mercury and Ketu.

The propitiation of Mars activises the vacant lagna. He becomes the significator of sex. His span is 6 years out of the 35 year cycle of planets.

Lord Hanuman is the deity of Positive Mars and the ghosts are of Negative Mars. Copper and coral are the metal and precious stones respectively. Honey and sweets are liked by him.

Remedies for Ills of Mars in Various houses.

In lagna

1. Do not accept any thing free of cost or in charity. Never tell a lie.
2. Ivory things will be harmful to the native.

In 2nd house

1. Keep a red colour handker-chief with you.
2. Keep deer skin in the house.
3. Distribute jaggery and wheat to children at noon.

In 3rd house

1. Keep ivory things with you.
2. Wear silver ring in the left hand.

In 4th house

1. Serve the monkeys, mother and sadhus.
2. Keep away from black or one eyed man or from him who has his affected limbs.
3. No trade or business in sugar or honey.

In the 5th house

1. Plant a neem tree in the house.
2. Good moral character.
3. Keep water at night below the head and drop it in the flower pot in the morning.

In the 6th house

1. Distribute salt on the birth of a male child.
2. Remedies of Saturn.

In the 7th house

1. Good moral character.
2. Give sweets to sister, daughter, father's sister, mother's sister and wife's sister.
3. Help the children of brother.
4. Never plant creeping plants.

In the 8th house

1. Blessings of widows.
2. Sweet loaves of bread for dogs. (use *tandoor*)
3. Remedies of Mars in 4th and 6th house simultaneously.

In the 9th house

1. Service of Bhabhi (brother's wife).
2. Obeying the elder brother.
3. Red colour cloth in the pocket.

In the 10th house.

1. Keep a pet deer.
2. The boiling milk should not overflow and fall on the fire.

In the 11th house

1. Keep *Sindoor* or honey in an earthen pot.

In the 12th house

1. Take honey the first thing in the morning.

General remedies

1. Fast on Tuesday.
2. Sindoor to Lord Hanuman.
3. Throw in the running water pulse of masoor, or honey or sindoor.
4. Service of brother.
5. Sleeping on deer skin.
6. Pure silver to be used.

MERCURY

Mercury is a small planet having vast potential to play mischief secretly. He is compared with a bat who lives in the dark hanging upside down. Mercury likewise loves to remain in the dark, and if possible, affect the native by ill designs secretly. If a case is to come up for decision on a particular day and if there is some body who will help him by taking a favourable decision, Mercury will create such circumstances suddenly that the officer favouring the person does not attend his duties and some other person who is not well disposed to the native decides the case adversely. In other words we can say that Mercury brings in the Providence suddenly to take an adverse decision.

Mercury is also considered to be the messenger of gods, that he does according to the message of some other planet who happens to be near him or influence him by virtue of being his sign dispositor. He becomes good in the company of good planets and bad in the company of bad planets. If the sign dispositor of Mercury happens to occupy the 9th house he fails to give any results. Except in 4th house Mercury always carries with him the effects of Rahu and Ketu. Mercury is generally a malefic in houses 3, 8, 9 and 12 and Rahu in houses 1, 5, 7, 8 and 11 is a malefic. If Rahu and Mercury happen to be posited in their malefic houses Mercury plays havocs. If the native does not get a jail term he will at least face a similar situation. He may lend himself in an assylum without any reason or rhyme. Steel ring on body will be providing protection. The steel ring should have no joint. If Mercury and Ketu are joined by aspect the former will give results as per his position and placement in the chart but Ketu will behave like Ketu in debility. Those suffering from the ills of Mercury should get their noses pierced as the ladies do for wearing ornaments. They should also keep their nose dry and clean. Keeping the teeth clean is also a valuable remedy. Service of sister, sister-in-law or of mother's sister will pay dividends.

Goddess Durga is the deity of this planet. Mercury represents the brain, teeth and nervous system. Publications, printing presses, journtalism are some of the relevant vocations of Mercury parrot, bat and goat are the animals. The relatives governed by

Mercury are father's sister, mother's sister. wife's sister, daughter and own sister.

Here for the sake of convenience we give tables showing how Mercury behaves in different houses.

Mercury in house	*Gives the results of*	*spoils the results of*
1.	Sun	Mars
2.	Jupiter	Venus
3.	Mars	Venus
4.	Moon	Moon
5.	Jupiter	Sun
6.	Ketu	Ketu, Mercury
7.	Venus	Venus
8.	Mars, Saturn	Mars
9.	Jupiter	Jupiter
10.	Saturn	Saturn
11.	Jupiter	Saturn
12.	Rahu	Rahu, Jupiter

Mercury in some cases helps the other planets.

Meucury in house	*Shall help*
1 to 2	Saturn
3 to 8	Sun
9 to 12	Saturn

Remedies for the ills of Mercury

I. In lagna

I. Do not take eggs. Do not be non veg.

2. No fishing.

In the 2nd house

1. Clean the teeth with alum.
2. Never domesticate parrot, goat or sheep.
3. Milk and rice for temples.

In the 3rd house

1. Durga Poojan or blessings of girls not attaining puberty.
2. Keep Moong in water in the night and feed pigeons in the morning.
3. Free distribution of asthma medicines.

In the 4th house

1. Do not domesticate parrot, goat or sheep.
2. Remedies of Sun.
3. Remedies of Jupiter.
4. No green colour at home, not even the plants.

In the 5th house

1. Use a belt.
2. Wear silver ring in left hand.

In the 6th house

1. Sister or daughter should not go in marriage in north side of the house.
2. Earthen pot filled with milk should be buried in uninhabited place.
3. As at No.2 under 6th house above.
4. Ganges water in a glass bottle having glass cover to be buried in the agricultural land.

In the 7th house

1. Daughter should be treated like the mother.
2. Wear a diamond or emerald ring.

In the 8th house

1. A silver ring in the nose of daughter.
2. Wear a black colour under wear (half pent)
3. Rain water to be kept on the roof.
4. No change in the place of worship at home.

In the 9th house

1. Wearing silver
2. Wear new clothes after washing them in river water or sprinkling the water.
3. No green colour.

In the 10th house

1. No money plant or *tulsi* plant in home.
2. No drinking wine or non vegetarianism and no fishing.
3. Remedies of Saturn

In the 11th house

1. Empty vessel should not be covered.
2. No planting of broad leafed trees.

In the 12th house

1. New unused earthen pitcher with cover to be dropped in running water.
2. Domesticating the dog but not of brown colour.
3. Durga pujan or blessings of girls not attaining puberty
4. Keeping the promise.
5. No ill word for any body.
6. Anger should be controlled.

General remedies

1. Fasting on Wednesdays.
2. Green things in alms or dropped in the running water.

3. Copper coin with a hole to be dropped in the running water.
4. Service of or domesticating goat and parrot.
5. Belt to be used.
6. Bangles and clothes of green colour to be given to eunuchs.
7. If Mercury is in debility the things of Mercury should be given in alms, but never should this be done when Mercury is in exaltation.
8. Blessings of daughter, sister, father's sister, mother's sister and wife's sister. They should also be helped to the extent possible.

SATURN

Saturn is the slowest moving planet. Its results are, therefore, felt for the period longer than of any other planet. His intensity is also more than that of any other planet. Due to these characteristics he is considered to have greatest Karmic influence on earth. While the facts remain unchallenged Saturn is never that great rascal as he is taken for. As the lord of 10th house he controls the destiny. If he is a malefic for some natives, it is because he awards the fruits according to the misdeeds of the native.

In fact Saturn has two aspects. He is a saint on the one hand leading life of extreme austerity and renunciation and on the other a great rogue who allows no respite to the sufferer. He becomes this or that according to the requirements of fate and destiny of the individual native. In Lal Kitab his good qualities are represented by Ketu and bad by Rahu. These nodes are virtually his agents who are poles apart from each other.

Saturn is considered to be the significator of vision in Lal Kitab. This is against the principles of general astrology. Perhaps the author means by vision the power of discrimination which can be granted to him due to his serious thoughtful nature. He has a power to identify the nature etc of every person easily and play his mischief accordingly if he is a malefic.

Saturn is considered to be a serpent. Rahu is its head or mouth and Ketu its tail. If Ketu is in earlier houses than Saturn, the latter becomes a great benefic. He always helps the native. If the position is otherwise Saturn becomes the most poisonous cobra. When Saturn is a benefic and if he occupies houses 2, 5, 9 or 12 he never gives bad results. Venus aspecting Saturn from earlier houses will affect the near relatives of the native, house and all the articles of Saturn. Saturn normally does not harm the children unless Jupiter and Venus or Mercury and Mars, both artificial Saturn, are together. Even the children shall be harmed particularly when Saturn occupies the 5th house or Mars and Mercury are there together. When Saturn is a malefic Rahu will be his agent for bad results. He becomes a great malefic if he has any connection with Rahu or Ketu. If Moon and Rahu occupy jointly or individually the 12th house Saturn shall always be a malefic. When Saturn co-occupies a house with two or more male planets he does not remain a malefic. He may not be a benefic in such a case. To give in charity the commodities of Saturn like the things made of iron or steel will be useful. Accompanied with female planets in houses 1,4,7, or 10 Saturn shall behave like Rahu and Ketu and will give bad results. If Saturn aspects female planets and his enemy planets together he will give adverse results in respect of the inimical planets. He spoils the results of the planets as given below –

Saturn in house	*Spoils the results of*
1.	Mars and Sun
3.	Mars
4.	Moon
5.	Sun
8.	Mars

Saturn never gives bad results when occupying houses ruled by Jupiter but Jupiter in the 10th house becomes debilitated and gives bad results. Mars is in a privileged position in the 10th house but Saturn in the 3rd house makes the native pauper and poor. Saturn in the 12th house ruled by Rahu is bad.

Bhairon is the deity of Saturn. Iron and steel are his metals. Coal, stones, salt, pepper urad (unwashed pulse), mustard oil, spirit and wine are his articles. Blacksmiths, carpenters, and cobblers are his vocations. Buffalo, fish, serpent scorpion, crow and kites are his birds and animals. Father's brothers are his relations. Keekar tree, dates, shoes and socks are also governed by Saturn.

Remedies for each house

In the lagna.

1. Serve the monkeys.
2. Pour milk with sugar in the roots of banyan tree and apply tilak of the moist mud there.
3. Do not tell a lie and have no evil eye on the things of others.

In the 2nd house

1. Apply tilak on the forehead of curd or milk.
2. Domesticate a grey buffalo.
3. Milk for serpent.

In the 3rd house

1. No wine or non vegetarianism.
2. No dark room in the end of the house.
3. No gate of the house towards East or South.
4. Remedies of Ketu.

In the 4th house

1. Protect the serpents and give milk to them.
2. Pour milk in the well

3. Food for buffalo, crows or helping the labourers.
4. One kilogram of wine to be thrown in the running water.
5. No green colour and do not wear clothes of black colour.

In the 5th house

1. Keep gold or *Kesar* on person.
2. Remedies of Mercury.
3. Take some almonds to the temple and bring back half of the them and keep them in white cloth at home.
4. Do not construct a house before 48 years of age.

In the 6th house

1. Do not purchase any new article of leather or iron. Old articles can be purchased.

In the 7th house

1. An earthen pot filled with honey should be kept in an uninhabited area.
2. Fill sugar in a bamboo flute and bury it in an uninhabited place.

In the 8th house

1. Keep on person a silver piece.
2. Protect the serpents and give milk to them.
3. No wine or non vegetarianism.

In the 9th house

1. Construct the last room of the house dark.
2. Do not store fuel etc. on the roof of the house.
3. Remedies of Jupiter.

In the 10th house

1. Remedies of Jupiter.

2. No construction of house before 48 years of age.
3. No wine or non vegetarianism.

In the 11th house

1. As at 3 under l0th house above.
2. The gate of the house should not be towards south.
3. Keep silver brick in the house.

In the 12th house

I. As at 3 under 10th house above.
2. No windows or gate in the last wall of the house.
3. Do not tell a lie.

General Remedies

1. Fastings on Saturdays.
2. Bhairon worship and giving wine to him in the temple of Bhairon.
3. Milk for the serpents.
4. Oil and wine to be distributed free.
5. Loaf of bread with mustard oil on it to be given to dogs and crows.

RAHU

Rahu is a node of Moon. His English name is Dragon's Head. In Lal Kitab also it is known by the same name. He is called to be an agent of Saturn. If Saturn is regarded as serpent Rahu is his hood or face. In other words Rahu is a malefic planet.

Rahu's colour is blue. The blue sky and the blue seas (that is deep seas who are depicted as blue in colour) are governed by Rahu. Jupiter is regarded as the air or wing which can go from higher to lower levels and vice-versa. Rahu in the 12th house which is ruled by Jupiter becomes stronger than Jupiter if both co-occupy the house. Jupiter there under such a condition becomes purely worldly man. Rahu does not allow him to go to higher domains. Rahu is such a mighty planet that the world is brought to its knees.

Rahu shall never be bad so long as the 4th house or Moon is not afflicted. He gives good results when Mars occupies house 12/3 or Sun and Mercury are in house No.3 or when he himself is posited in the 4th house. He becomes good when he has connections with Mercury, that is, he is with Mercury or is aspected by him. If Rahu occupies the houses earlier than those occupied by Saturn the latter will do things at his bidding. In the vice versa position Saturn becomes stronger and Rahu acts as his agent. He afflicts Moon but not when both of them are posited in the same house. If Rahu is a malefic his evil effects shall continue till the age of 42 of the native. He is generally a malefic when Sun and Venus transit a house together. He is a great malefic when Saturn and Sun transit the house together. Even Mars in such a case shall behave as Mars negative. If Rahu along with his enemies (Sun. Mars or Venus) aspects Ketu the bad effects will be upon the male children and upon the articles of trade and relatives concerning Ketu. If Rahu is connected with Sun by association or by aspect he will spoil the house he is posited in and also the adjoining next house. During the bad effects of Rahu the southern gate of the house shall play havocs. There should, therefore, be no gate on the southern side of the house.

When Rahu gives bad results following remedies may be generally useful.

1. Remedies involving silver when mental peace is disturbed.
2. Pulse of Masoor (red colour) may be given to the sweeper or he should be helped in other ways.
3. Barley or wheat equal in weight of the sick person to be dropped in the running water.

4. Barley should be kept under the bed on the side of the head in the night and distributed in the morning to the poor.
5. To solve the problem of business or trade with the Government charcoal equal to the weight of the native should be dropped in the running water.

Out of 35 year cycle Rahu has a span of 6 years. Goddess Saraswati is his deity. Lead and Gomed are his metals and precious stone respectively. Barley, mustard, moong are the articles concerning Rahu. Memory and imagination are his qualities. Electrical implements and machinery, blue colour, toilet, chimney and trousers are governed by him. The parents of wife and mother are also under his domain.

Remedies for each house

In the lagna

1. Wheat, Jaggery and brass should be given in alm or to the temple.
2. Silver piece (square or rectangular having the same thickness every where should be worn around the neck).
3. Taking milk bath.

In the 2nd house

1. Keep small silver balls in the pocket.
2. Haldi or kesar tilak on forehead.
3. Wearing gold ornaments
4. Keep silver or water in the north-west side of house.

In the 3rd house

1. Do not keep ivory or any thing made of ivory.
2. Remedies of Moon.

In the 4th house

1. Taking holy bath in Ganges at Hardwar.

2. The dirty water should not be stagnant in the house or near the four walls of the house.
3. No kitchen under the stair case.

In the 5th house

1. Keep a solid silver elephant toy.
2. Marrying your wife two times.
3. No second marriage.

In the 6th house

1. Domesticate a black dog.
2. Keep black glass windows at home or at office. 3. Keep small lead balls in the pocket.

In the 7th house

1. No dog in the house.
2. Keep silver brick in the house.
3. Throw coconut in the running water.

In the 8th house

1. Drop 8 lead coins every year in the running water till the age of 42.
2. Silver piece of the same thickness in the pocket.

In the 9th house

1. Living in joint family.
2. Wear gold.
3. Bowing head in the temple.

In the 10th house

1. Always keep cap or something on head. Never be bare headed.
2. Remedies of Mars.

3. Wearing gold ornaments.
4. Keep silver or water in the north-west side of house.

In the 11th house

1. Silver on head.
2. Taking milk in silver vessel.
3. Use a silver container for cigarettes or have a silver pipe.
4. No weapons in the house or on person.
5. Four kilos of lead and one dry coconut to be dropped in the running water.

In the 12th house

1. Sugar and *saunf* to be kept under the pillow.
2. Solid silver elephant toy in the house.
3. A dark room in the end of the house.

General for all houses

1. Saraswati poojan.
2. Never accept electrical items, steel vessels or blue clothes.
3. Kanya daan.
4. Wearing Gomed.
5. Live in joint family.
6. Never use tobacco

KETU

Ketu is treated as a Darwesh or a spiritualist concerned with the upper world. He stands for final emancipation from this material world. He is the messenger of kindness and karaka of journeys and travels and helpful to the last. The three parts of Ketu are Jupiter, Mars and Mercury. The three dogs associated with Ketu are (1) brother at the house of sister after marriage, (2) the son-in-law at the house of his father-in-law and (3) son of daughter at maternal uncle's house. The dog of Ketu is white and black. Whiteness stands for the day and blackness for the night. In other words Ketu is strong both by night and day. If there is red colour it represents Mercury. The effects of such a dog be those of Mercury and the duration that of Ketu. When Ketu is giving bad results the native should not let out his secrets to any body or bemoan his ill luck before any body because then the effects will be manifold. For bad effects of Ketu the planets in 10th house will give an indication. When the bad effets are on the health of the native remedies of Moon will be helpful. Ketu also affects the male progeny. When that is so a blanket given to the temple will be helpful. When there is trouble in the foot or urinary trouble on account of Ketu the white silken thread should be tied around both the toes of the feet. Ketu is also treated as the cot (sleeping bed) and the bed coming in dowry at the time of marriage is governed by Ketu. This bed should be used particularly at the time of the birth of the child by child's mother. So long as this continues to be done Ketu will generally not be bad.

When Ketu is bad or malefic he affects others adversely. He becomes bad or papi or sinful when he comes in contact with Rahu or Saturn by way of aspect or association. Rahu as such shall never be with Ketu but the group of artificial planets constituting Rahu may be posited in the same house. There shall be no deaths of any relative on account of bad Ketu. The miseries shall be of other kinds. Bad Ketu generally afflicts the residential house, children and the female folks. When Jupiter or Sun are afflicted by their inimical planets they will give bad effects in respect of Ketu. When Ketu is bad it generally affects the children. If they suffer from *Sookha* disease mud from river or nallah or any other mud should be applied to the whole body and after it gets dried up, say in half an hour or so, give the child a bath and clean the mud. This should continue without a break for 43 days. The child shall start recovering.

Lord Ganesha is the deity. *Lahsonia* is the precious stone. Bananas yellow, lime, black and white til are the articles of Ketu. Two coloured dog (white and black), mouse, any dog, pig, donkey and lizard are the animals of Ketu. Son, daugther's son and sister's son are the relatives governed by Ketu.

General Remedies for each house

In the lagna

1. Domesticate a white and black dog or serve such a dog.
2. Not to live in the last house of the lane.
3. Remedies of Moon.
4. Keep red coloured cloth in the pocket.

In the 2nd house

1. Maintain good character.
2. Serving the girls particularly of the ages below nine years.

In the 3rd house

1. Wear gold
2. To avoid any mishap in the journey or loss in journey drop articles of Sun and Moon in the running water.
3. Jupiter's articles to be dropped in the running water.

In the 4th house

1. Giving articles of Jupiter in charity to the places of worship.
2. Serving the family priest.

In the 5th house

1. Propitiate Jupiter and make him good.
2. Articles of Saturn should not be kept closed. Iron box should not be locked. Iron locks should not be kept locked.

In the 6th house

1. The ring received as dowry should be worn in the left hand.
2. The same as at (1) under 5th house above.

In the 7th house

1. Four pieces of charcoal to be dropped in the running water for four days.
2. four limes to the dropped in running water for 4 days.

In the 8th house

I. Black and white blanket as charity to the places of worship.
2. Pieces of black and white blanket with the things of planets posited in the same house, should be buried in the crematorium.

In the 9th house

1. Gold in the ears like gold rings or tops etc.
2. Keeping gold brick in the house.

In the 10th house

1. Keeping milk and honey under the foundation stone of the house.
2. Keep a pet dog after 48 years of age.
3. Keep honey in a silver vessel.
4. Good conduct and character.

In the 11th house

1. Keep a black pet dog.

In the 12th house

1. Suck the thumb dipped in milk. (if there is a male child already).
2. White and black dog.

General Remedies for all the 12 houses

1. Fasting on Ganesha Chaturthi and Ganesha Poojan.
2. *Til,* lime and bananas etc. to be given in charity.
3. White and black pet dog in the house or feeding such a dog daily.
4. Good moral character and conduct.
5. Sour things to be given to female children below the age of nine years.
6. Black and white til to be dropped in running water.

5

Mental Powers, Vibrations, Houses of the Chart and the Planets

It is well known that human mind has a number of divisions. The first division is the right and left sides of it. The right side is governed by the marks on the left hand and the left side of the mind can be judged from the marks on the right hand. Generally speaking it is the left side of the mind which is active. As the left side of the mind is judged from the right hand in palmistry it is the right hand that is mostly judged. That is why this part of the mind we have started using due to our present circumstances and experiences.

It is a general assertion that the left hand of the ladies and right hand of males should be judged. There is no such rule in the Lal Kitab. This presumption or assertion might have some relevance in those days when females were not supposed to be the active partners of their counterparts. Under such circumstances there was no opportunity for the women to adjust themselves. They enjoyed or suffered with their husbands what came their way. Today it is not so. Women are equal partners in all the departments of life, not only as wives but as equal partners or some times even as competitors. The study of right hand of males and left of females does not appear to be having any validity.

Mental vibrations are ruled by Rahu because he is the Dragon's head and governs it in his own right. In order to study the nature of vibrations we may first study Rahu vis-a-vis the houses and the planets. For human beings self always comes before anything else. What he does and how he acts is always according to the contingencies facing him. Even in such innocent actions as looking at a group photograph involving self or some near and dear ones he first searches for his photo or that of his near and dear one who happens to be in the group. If this be the thing an active individual be if he or she, shall be judged by the same hand. Today all are active. Therefore the question of studying different hands for different persons does not probably arise.

The entire mind has been divided into 42 parts. Each part is connected with one or the other planet. In some cases more than one planet have their sway over the same part. These parts are divided into twelve houses of the birth chart. The planet transiting those houses activates those impulses or qualities of mind.

Mental Division	*Qualities of the Division*	*Connected with House No.*
1	Connected with Venus. Attraction in the first instance and infatuation subsequently called love. This is with opposite sex starting at the age of 16 and lasting till the age of 36 years. Connected with Saturn. It is virtually no love for love but love for selfish ends if Saturn is bad. There is sympathy when Saturn is good.	1
37	Concerning Saturn. Love for the abstract.	1
2	Concerning Jupiter. Desire for getting married. Love for sex from 37 years to 70 years of age.	2
38	Concerning jupiter. Power to learn many languaes and strong power of expression	2

Mental Division	*Qualities of the Division*	*Connected with House No.*
3	Concerning Venus. Love for children and parents.	2
	Concerning Mars. Attraction for the sex remaining upto 75 years of age.	3
10	Concerning Mercury. Taste of the tongue. Good digestion.	3
27, 39	Concerning Mars. Power of deep thinking and trying to reach the bottom of things.	3
4, 28, 41	Concerning Moon. Power to make friends and meet people. This includes attraction, love and infatuation also if need be and also the ability to ignore the shortcomings of others and following only good points. Sharp memory for names, dates and events.	3
	Concerning Mars negative. Family life etc. spoilt due to love and affection.	4
5, 15	Concerning Jupiter. Love for the country and patriotism. Self respect but not insulting any body for the sake of self respect.	5
20	Concerning Sun. Maintaining others' respect and doing his own duties truthfully and honestly.	5
22	Concerning Jupiter. Intelligence	5
29	Understanding the man and using him for own purpose and interests.	5

Mental Division	*Qualities of the Division*	*Connected with House No.*
41	Realising good points of others. Never sacrificing good qualities for selfish ends.	5
6	Concerning Ketu. Firmness in interest and love. Prepared to do any work and leaving it without its completion.	6
	Concerning Venus. Weakness in sexual affairs.	6
16	Concerning Ketu. Not to be distrubed in the face of disappointment and failures. Keeping busy in doing the work in hand, whether good or bad.	6
23	Love for beauty and charms. Lady should be beautiful and charming with no regards to her qualities etc.	6
30	Knowing the real nature of man. Behaviour tit for tat.	6
42	Concerning Mercury. Extreme adjustments with every body and changing the self according to the circumstances.	6
7	Concerning Venus and Mercury. Wish to live long. No idea of living better.	7
24	Concerning Venus. No body should rise higher than myself.	7
31	Power of discrimination	7
8	Concerning Mars Positive and Sun. Firm in actions. No deviations in the	

Mental Division	*Qualities of the Division*	*Connected with House No.*
	face of disappointments and failures and competence to change the direction of events.	8
14	Concerning Mars negative. Thinking every body inferior to his own self.	8
24	Copying others. Master in the art of mimicry etc.	8
32	Concerning Saturn. Good arrangements of things. Every thing at its right place. Good in appearance and behaviors but not what he appears at the surface.	8
9	Concerning Saturn. Revengeful and never forgetting. He would himself take the revenge failing which shall ask his children to do it.	9
19	Religious and spiritual good character. If the house is weak he will be a non believer.	9
26	Concerning Jupiter. Cheerful, playing intellectual pranks.	9
33	Concerning Mercury. Principal man. Interest in geometry etc. self imposed limitations.	9
13	Concerning Saturn. Intelligent. Not dependent on luck; but active and planning even for the adversity in time. Long term planning.	10
34	Concerning Mars negative. A cheat and betrayer. Good memory of places and surroundings.	10

Mental Division	*Qualities of the Division*	*Connected with House No.*
11	Concerning Saturn. Amassing wealth and wishing to construct big houses and buildings. Here are three types. (1) Amassing wealth for futrue use. (2) Wealth for the sake of wealth. Extremely miser. (3) Stealing other's wealth and using it immediately.	11
35	Good memory for dates and events, particularly the political events.	11
36	Lost in the past keeping his cards close to chest.	11
12	Does not say what he wishes to do unless he decides to do it. Doing things cleverly and even clandestinely and keeping his intentions secret.	12

6

Parental Afflictions

(Rin Pitri)

It is often seen that we suffer in this world apparently for no fault of ours. If the sufferings are common to a number of persons of the same family even over a gap of generations we can reasonably assume that those sufferings are the result of some misdeeds, or to put it mildly, wrongs done by the ancestors of that family. Amongst the ancestors may be the parents or some relatives of the native.

It may look strange or unbelievable that we should suffer for the crimes or sins of some body else, but it is true. A child inherits property from parents. He also comes to be the owner of some things given to him by way of will or legacies etc., and he does enjoy them to the full. If he can inherit material things why can not he inherit the liabilities of others. It is not only these liabilities and property, but also the nature, of course, to some limited extent, of his parents. Thus inheriting the curse of our ancestors is quite reasonable and logical.

Parental afflictions or curses go by the name of Rin Pitri (ऋण पितृ) or the debts of parents. we have to pay back what our parents owed to some body in their life time. We do not know what the debt or liability actually our fore-fathers owed with the result that we cannot repay that loan. In such case we repay by sufferings or by penance. The penance are called the remedies.

Every planet has his houses of ownership and houses of natural significations. If some enemy of a planet occupies one of such houses of the former we have sufferings. If similar phenomenon happens over a number of persons in the same family we can reasonably assume that the sufferings are the results of some curse.

Here are three birth charts. They are of father, son and the grandson, that is, the persons belonging to three generations. In chart A Jupiter occupies his own house the 9th, but is afflicted by

A

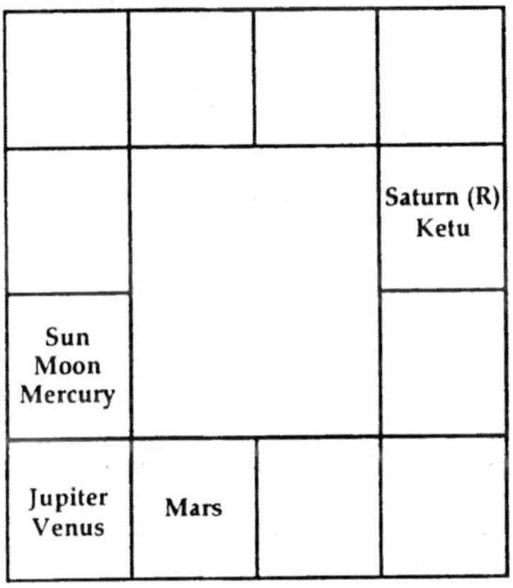

A

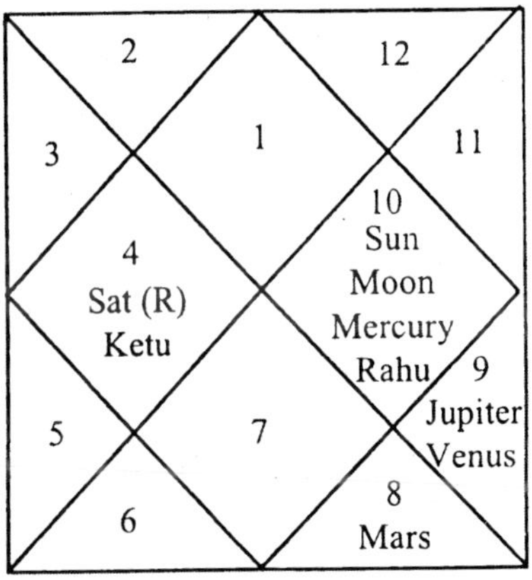

B

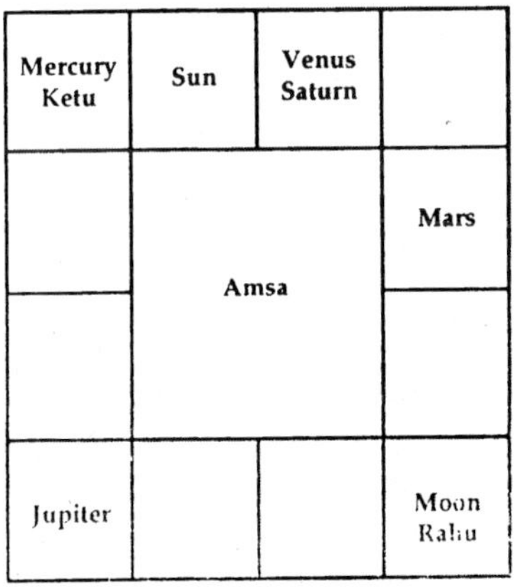

B

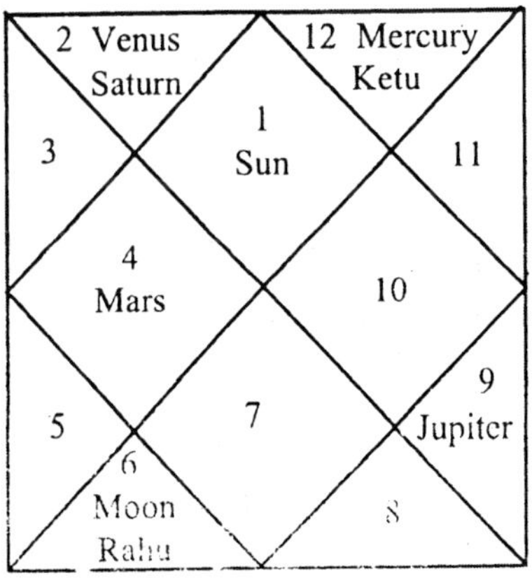

C

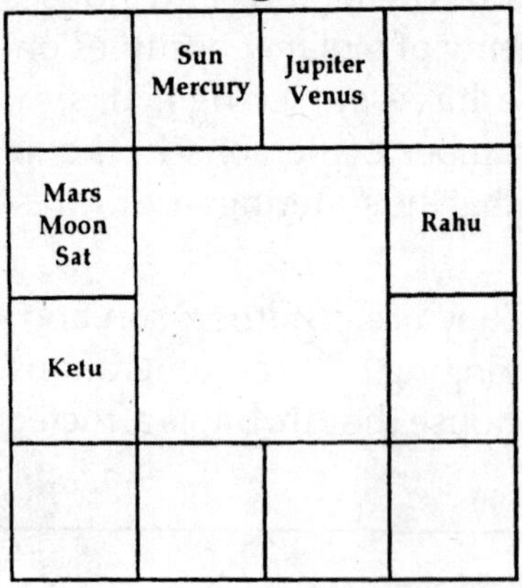

C

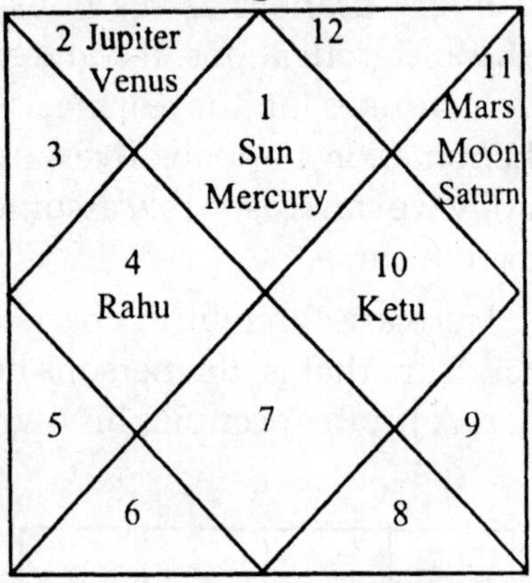

Venus as they are inimical. In the same chart house No.4 whose ruler Moon is occupied by his enemy Ketu and Saturn. In chart B Jupiter occupies the 9th house which is his own but Mercury occupies the 12th house whose lord is also Jupiter. Moon the lord of 4th house in chart B is afflicted by Rahu. In chart C Jupiter the 9th lord occupies 2nd house with his enemy Venus. House No.2 is the house of natural signification of Jupiter. Even the 4th house in chart C is afflicted by Rahu. As the afflictions are similar in three charts belonging to persons of three generations we can take it that the sufferings are due to Parental curse or Rin Pitri. In Lal Kitab Jupiter represents father and Moon mother. The natives are carrying over their heads the burden of the curses of both parents.

The above three charts have been judged on the basis of general theories enunciated in Lal Kitab. There are certain combinations of planets which indicate the curses. In such cases Mercury gets more importance than any other planet. Mercury is supposed to have power of moulding the effects of any of the planets. Friendship or enmity is not the concern here. Mercury in such cases becomes a matching planet and as such seizes the opportunity to inflict harm.

Here are the cases where Mercury inflicts pain when, the other planets occupy the 9th house:

1. Jupiter occupies 9th house and Mercury the 12th house.
2. Sun occupies 9th house and Mercury the 5th house.
3. Moon occupies 9th house and Mercury the 4th house.
4. Mars occupies 9th house and Mercury the 1st or 8th house.
5. Venus occupies 9th house and Mercury the 2nd or 7th house.
6. Satum occupies 9th house and Mercury the 10th or 11th house.
7. Rahu occupies 9th house and Mercury the 12th house.
8. Ketu occupies 9th house and Mercury the 6th house.

Any of the above position will point out to the likelihood of some parental curse. In time and suitable remedial measures should be adopted for the rescue. Here we have taken the planets occupying 9th house only. Mercury by becoming a matching planet can undo the good results of the relevant planet. Now we are giving some planetary combinations involving house.

Planet in houses other than	*Afflicting planet in houses*
1. Jupiter 2, 3, 5, 6, 9 and 12	Saturn as a malefic in 2
2. Jupiter 2, 3, 5, 6, 9 and 12	Venus as a malefic in 5
3. Jupiter 2, 3, 5, 6, 9 and 12	Mercury as a malefic in 9
4. Jupiter 2, 3, 5, 6, 9 and 12	Rahu as a malefic in 12
5. Jupiter 2, 3, 5, 6, 9 and 12	Mercury/Venus as a malefic in 3/6
6. Jupiter 2, 3, 5, 6, 9 and 12	Saturn as a malefic in 3/6

7. Sun in houses other than 1 and 11 and Venus/Rahu/Ketu in 5th house.
8. Moon in house other than 4, and Venus, Mercury and Saturn in 4th house.
9. Venus in houses other than 1 and 8 and any of or all of Sun, Moon and Rahu in 2nd or 7th house.

10. Mars in house other than 7th and Mercury and Ketu in houses 1st or 8th.
11. Mercury in houses other than 2 and 12 and Moon in houses 3, 6.
12. Saturn in houses other than 3 and 4 and Sun, Moon and Mars in 10th or 11th house.
13. Rahu in houses other than 6th and Sun, Venus and Mars in 12th house.
14. Ketu in houses other than 2 and Moon and Mars in 6th house.

Merely the above position of planets is not a sure indication of parental curse. We have to see something more for a final declaration of our judgement. There should also be a simultaneous affliction of houses 2, 5, 9 and 12. If that is not so despite the above planetary combinations there is no case of parental curse. Lal Kitab specifically refuses to consult the progressed horoscope in this respect. Only birth chart has to be judged in this respect.

After listing the various combinations we give here the remedies provided in Lal Kitab for the planets.

1. Jupiter

All the members of the family and blood relations, should donate one paisa each and give to the temple on one and the same day.

2. Sun

A yajna should be performed and the expenses should be equally divided between the blood relations.

3. Moon

Equal weight of silver should be collected from all the family relations, blood relations and dropped in the flowing water of a river on one day and at the same time.

4. Venus

One hundred cows should be fed sumptuously and the expenditure divided equally amongst the blood relations of the native.

5. Mercury

One kauri each from members of the family (blood relations wherever they may be living) should be collected and burnt at one place. The ashes of the burnt kauris should be thrown in the running water of any river. None of the members snould be present at the place of throwing. The kauris should be of yellow colour. (Kauris are used in the game known as chopad. It is an indigenous game which was very common in olden days).

6. Mars

In the village there may be one shop where the owner of the shop follows the vocation of Mars. One paisa should be collected from each member of blood relations and paid to the shop owner and he should be asked to work freely for some of his customers to the extent of money given to him. The vocations of Mars are Iron smiths, fixing iron in the hoofs of horses, hakeems (medical practitioners) and craftsmen etc.

7. Saturn

Fish brought from one hundred places should be fed on one day at the same time and the expenses shared equally by all the members of the family, that is, by the blood" relations.

8. Rahu

One coconut collected from each of the members (blood relations) should be thrown in the running water of any river on one day at the same time.

9. Ketu

One hundred dogs should be fed the good food on one day and the expenses divided among all the blood relations.

Note

1. Blood relations include even the sisters, daughters and their children. Sometimes some of the relatives may refuse to pay their share of expenses because of having no faith in such things. In such cases the native may tell them that the

parental curse shall continue on them who do not share the expenses on account of the remedies and that they would continue to suffer on account of the curse. Those who have shared the expenses are free from that curse. In some cases the native may feel like helping those relatives who do not pay their share of expenses. In such cases the native has to pay 10 times the share of those relatives. If he does so the non-paying members shall also be freed from the curse.

Identification of the person whose curse the members are suffering from

If it is desired to identify the particular ancestor whose curse is tormenting the members we can do so by examining the afflicting and the afflicted planets and the houses they occupy.

1. Venus, Mercury and Rahu in houses No.2, 5, 9, 12

Paternal curse for change of family priest or the neighbours may have destroyed some peepal tree etc.

2. Venus or Rahu or Ketu in house No. 5

Personal curse. Irreligious actions.

Indications : There may be Agni kund under-ground of the house or many openings in the roof for the entry of light etc.

3. Ketu in house No.4

Maternal Curse : On getting a child the native might have started troubling his mother or may not have helped her in her troubles and miseries.

Indications : The native may be throwing the dust and dirt of his house in the river, well or some flowing water.

4. Sun, Rahu and Moon in houses 2 or 7

Wife's curse : Women beating in the family or killing some pregnant lady for some benefits.

Indications : People may be averse to keep pet animals particularly the pet cow.

5. Mercury or Ketu in houses 1 or 8

Curse of the relatives : Poisoning somebody, setting the new house on fire or killing a pregnant cow or buffalo.

Indications : Against the relatives, hating to meet them. Not celebrating the children's births or the family festivals.

6. Moon in house 3 or 6

Curse of daughter or sister

Indications : Selling the innocent children of any sex or exchange of them which has been legalised by undesirable means.

7. **Sun, Moon Mars in houses 10 or 1**

Curse due to tyranny :

Indications : Main gate of the house may generally be towards south or taking the land of issueless persons and constructing house etc.

8. Sun, Moon or Mars in 12th house

Curse of children who were not allowed to be born.

Indication : Dirty water of the house flowing down the main entrance of the house

9. Moon or Mars in 6th house

Dargahi Curse or Natural Curse :

Indication : Killing or getting killed the male progeny of others or killing or getting killed the dogs or harming or killing the relations pertaining to Ketu.

We have given above the indications of various curses as mentioned in the Lal Kitab. It would be observed that they are quite out-dated. The sewage system of olden days was not the same as we have it today. The dirty water flowed through very small over ground gutters. We do not have that system these days. Similarly there is the question of main gate of buildings. It was easier to have the main entrance to any side of the house in olden days. Today we have houses on both sides of the roads or by lanes. The sides or the direction of main gates depend upon many factors. There is a planning. In order to make them useful in present day conditions we have to update them which needs careful study and research on Lal Kitab.

As regards the indications of the type of Pitri Rina there are also indications to show the affliction of planets. While the competent astrologers can find out the affliction of this or that planet by judging the birth charts the lay man needs some non-technical knowledge to identify the afflicted planet. As the behaviour of planets remains generally set under given circumstances a list of some very common events or happenings have been given below to indicate the affliction of any particular planet. On the basis of those general events one can, to some extent, arrive at conclusions regarding the affliction.

It may be mentioned here that the planet, whose houses of ownership are occupied by the enemy planet, is to be taken as afflicted. By way of example if Moon or Mars occupy 6th house in a chart they are afflicting Ketu. Moon in house 3 afflicts Mercury.

Afflicted Sun as indicator

When afflicted Sun is the indicator the unfortunate events will take place early in life, that is, in the youthful days of the native. He will rise in status, social or in the Government employment and go on rising. Suddenly there may be a stroke of misfortune when all his earnings are lost due to one reason or the other. There may be serious illness or some chronic diseases and the money has to be spent on them. This may happen when the child is eleven months old or is attaining eleven years of age.

Afflicted Moon as the indicator

When the native is associated with animals giving milk he starts suffering. All his riches and wealth starts disappearing because of unforeseen and unavoidable circumstances. The first casualty in such cases is the education. If some body in such cases tries to help the native he is himself rendered incapable to do it.

Afflicted Mars as the indicator

Just as adulthood sets in the person he starts gaining name, fame and honour and those who try to place hurdles are crushed under feet mercilessly. Assured success eludes just at the eleventh hour the man not only gets disappointment but also stroke of other misfortunes simultaneously.

Afflicted Mercury as the indicator

This relates to the timings of the birth or marriage of a daughter or sister. The misfortune strikes the native at such auspicious time and he is all gone. Sometimes this happens at the time of birth of a male child. Even the richest families have been made paupers if no human lights fade away. The reason could never be known.

Afflicted Jupiter as an indicator

Afflicted Jupiter's havocs appear with the black hair turning grey. It was all very happy a time till every body was young and his or her hair were dark. Life was smooth and comfortable but the moment some body's hair on the head started greying every thing turned to ashes. The yellow metal gold overnight turned into black iron and iron transformed itself into white ashes. Those which were the sources of name, fame and honour became the means of dishonour and unfounded rumours of allegations.

Afflicted Venus as an indicator

This starts with the marriage of some family member. On one side there are grand preparations for marriage and on the other side there happens something which introduces, or rather substitutes, elements of extreme sorrow. Some body suddenly dies in the family or rests on death bed finally to say good bye to all of them. Marriage party is transformed into a sorrow party.

Afflicted Saturn as indicator

It is just when God granted the opportunity of enjoying the fruits of one's actions heavy clouds of misfortune burst upon the family. There was a fire in the house or some accidents which crippled the native and enjoyers became the mourners. Those who were not even remotely responsible were accused for the catastrophe.

Afflicted Rahu as the indicator

Suddenness is the feature of Rahu. Every thing happens in the twinkle of an eye. There is either some short circuit or some unforeseen mishap which brings down the whole premises of good luck and happiness like a pack of cards. Justice begets injustice every where. Charges of misappropriation, theft, and what not, are labelled against the native and bring unfounded sentences on the subjects or the native.

Afflicted Ketu as indicator

The misfortune falls generally on the male children. Either there are no male children or if some are born they die soon or become crippled and invalid.

The above are only some of the indications which may remind us that there is something wrong somewhere. No exhaustive list can be prepared of such events. Recurrence of a similar type of events will bring to light that some thing is basically wrong with the family. The common source of common misfortunes can be found only in the common ancestory which may be called the parental curses or the parental afflictions.

The afflictions may be brought about by Mercury or any other malefic and inimical planets. Here are some of such planetary combinations. Mercury has been specifically named above because Mercury is considered to be a strong planet and can move the mountains. Each planet has his own houses. If the particular planet is in house No.9 and Mercury occupies any house of that planet there is an indication of parental curse or affliction.

7

Sickness and Diseases

Sicknesses and diseases are the normal features of human life. Some sicknesses merely come and go bearing no or insignificant effect upon the health of the native. Some are a little more intense. They do go but leave the native in very bad shape. There are still others which do come but do not go without taking their toll. Whatever be their nature they all are resources of worry. This is particularly so during the present times of prohibitive prices of everything including the medicines, medical consultations and medical attendance. The native and all his relatives seek light to dispel those unfortunate clouds of misery. The chart of the native comes ready at hand to know, if possible, the ultimate results of the misery and misfortune. While examining the chart we see the planetary positions and how they stand vis-a-vis the health of the native. Normal aspects of the planets have already been given elsewhere. We shall discuss some special conditions here.

The planets occupying houses 3 and 5 from each other become mutual friends and help each other. This temporal relationship is irrespective of their natural relationship. The planets occupying houses 5 and 7 behave a little differently. The planets in house No.5 have a particular signification of the affairs of the house. If they are giving good results to that house they will have bad influence over the affairs of house No.7 from them. If they are giving bad results in the house of their occupation they will have good influence over the affairs of 7th house. The planets in houses 6 and 8 will always be clashing and their behaviour will be inimical. In other words they will adversely affect the affairs of the two houses. The planets in houses 7 and 9 will be generally friendly or inimical as per their natural relationship. The planets in houses 8 and 10 will be inimical to each other. Judge the condition when house No.9 is occupied by Saturn and house No.6 is occupied (10th house from 9th house) by Mercury. Saturn in 9th house is a boon for the native. Mercury is in his own as well as his house of exaltation. Mercury is also a friend of Saturn. Despite all this Saturn will spoil the results of 6th house. The relations signified by 6th house, that is, the maternal uncles will have the kicks of Saturn and if they have a trade or business of the articles related to Saturn it will be doomed. Saturn will be good for the native and his elders signified by the 9th house. There shall be no bad effect on the native and his relations signified by the 9th house. Mercury will have no bad effect on Saturn because there are only 2 houses in between Mercury and Saturn. Here it may be remembered that the 3rd house does not mean the same thing as it means in natural astrology. The third house here means that there are three houses in between the houses occupied by the planets. Another point worth remembering is that the earlier houses aspect the later houses with a few exceptions. House No.8 has a backward aspect on house No.2. This is, however, not applicable to the planets who are sleeping or inert. They have their aspects both way that is both backward and forward.

After discussing these general conditions we come to the subject of illness and how it comes about. The basis for the examination here shall not be the birth chart but the annual progressed chart called the varshaphala.

Affliction of house No.3 in the birth chart shall set the ball rolling. If house No.3 is vacant the affliction or otherwise of 8th house will be the indicator. If house No.8 is also unoccupied we look to the 5th house for our purpose. If this house is also unoccupied the results can be known from house No. 11. If all of them remain unoccupied by any planet the position of the 4th house will give the position.

Sickness will start from the affliction of 8th house. Houses 2 and 4 will provide the handle. In other words we first judge house No.8 or the other houses as serially noted above. If there is affliction we judge houses 2 and 4 to see the type of illness. For the speed of illness, quick or slow, house No.10 will be relevant. When once the illness starts house No.5 will tell us the ability of the native to meet the expenses and 3rd house will say whether the same is mortal or not. House No.3 is a hurdle to the events of 8th house as stated above. The planets in houses 6 and 8 are always clashing and inimical. House No. 11 is in a position to afflict house No.3. If house No.3 is afflicted the position will depend upon the position of Moon. If Moon occupies the 4th house and Rahu and Ketu occupy either houses 2 and 8 or 6 and 12 the sickness will not be fatal. It will have no effect on the longevity of the native.

Bad times start with the afflictions of 8th house but the handle shall be provided by house No.2. We, therefore, judge 2nd house in the first instance. If house No.2 is occupied by planets mutually inimical there shall be a turmoil. The planets in this house are aspected by the planets in house No.8. If planets in the two houses are inimical then also there shall be bad results. If house No.10 is unoccupied there will be no effect of illness or there shall be no illness immediately. The native may fall ill when any of the malefic planet in the chart transits the 3rd or 9th house. For ill effects, Rahu or Ketu will be the main culprits. To know their results, better examine the position of Mercury and Jupiter. The former will indicate the nature of Rahu and the later that of Ketu. As for relief we again go to 8th house. The planets that are poisoning the 2nd house by their backward aspect on the house need propitiation. We have to do the remedies relating to the planet in 8th house. This shall be keeping the sickness in check. They will not give final cure. For final cure we see the bad planets in the 5th house. The remedies concerning the malefic planet in the 5th house will give the final cure. In short, we have to apply the remedies of planets in houses 8 and 5 of the chart. If house No.5 is vacant there is no possibility of illness. If there is some illness it will merely come and go. It shall have no or very little effect on health of the native.

If the 3rd house is occupied by Rahu or Ketu and house No.8 is also giving bad results the planets in house No.3 will get help from the planets in the 12th house irrespect of their natural inimical relationship.

If in the birth chart Sun and Venus or Sun and Jupiter are posited in the 5th house health of the native is likely to suffer when Venus or Rahu or Ketu transit the lagna. If Venus or Rahu or Ketu are in 5th house the health will suffer when Sun or Jupiter transit the lagna. The ill health shall continue till the birth of a child to the native provided Jupiter occupies house No.5 in the birth chart.

Illnesses signified by Planets

Sun : Palpitation of heart, Insanity, epilepsy, paralysis, Blood pressure if Mercury occupies house 6 or 12.

Moon : Heart diseases, eye troubles.

Mars : Diseases of stomach, cholera, liver.

Mercury : Small pox, diseases of skull and scalp, trouble of nerves, teeth or tongue. Blood pressure when Mercury is in 12th house and Sun in 6th house.

Jupiter : Breathing troubles, and troubles of lungs. Asthma

Venus : Skin diseases, itching etc. Piercing of the nose as ladies do for wearing ornaments in nose will be helpful.

Saturn : Eye-sight or vision, cough of every kind.

Rahu : Fevers, Mental diseases, Plague, accidents.

Ketu : Trouble in limbs, general eruptions, goitre, venereal diseases, ear troubles, spinal cord,

Jupiter, Rahu or Jupiter, Mercury : Asthma and breathing troubles

Rahu, Ketu, Kahu, Moon : Piles Pneumonia, insanity

Jupiter, Rahu, Sun, Venus or Mercury

Jupiter : T.B., Asthma.

Moon and Mercury, Mars, Saturn, Venus, Rahu : Glandular troubles, Blood troubles, Impotence.

Before proceeding further in our studies it would be better to discuss a case to make the concept clearer. Here is the birth chart of a female native.

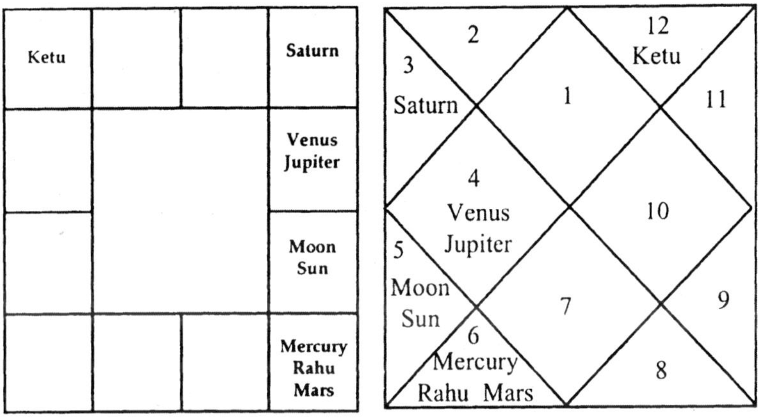

House 6 and 8 are mysterious houses dealing with unforeseen circumstances. House No. 8 is unoccupied. House No.6 is occupied by Mercury the lord of the house, Mars the lagna lord and Rahu. The planets are all inimical. Venus and Jupiter the 7th and the 12th lords respectively occupy the 4th house. They will not be able to spoil the results of 4th house so long as Moon does not occupy any of the angular house which he is fortunately not occupying at the time of birth. The vulnerability is, however, there because the planets in the 4th house are inimical to each other and also malefics. They shed away their enmity in the 4th house and become neutral to each other. This neutrality does not mean that they do not spoil the results of the house, but simply that they do not come in the way of each other. This again shows the vulnerabilityof the 4th house. The house can get assistance from 11th house planets; but unfortunately there is no planet in the 11th house. This again is the indication of the weakness of the

4th house. There is an indication that the heart of the native is likely to suffer when the transits of planets are unfavourable. The native suddenly fell seriously ill in 1995. The horary chart was prepared for the study of the trouble and causes, if any. The horary chart is given below.

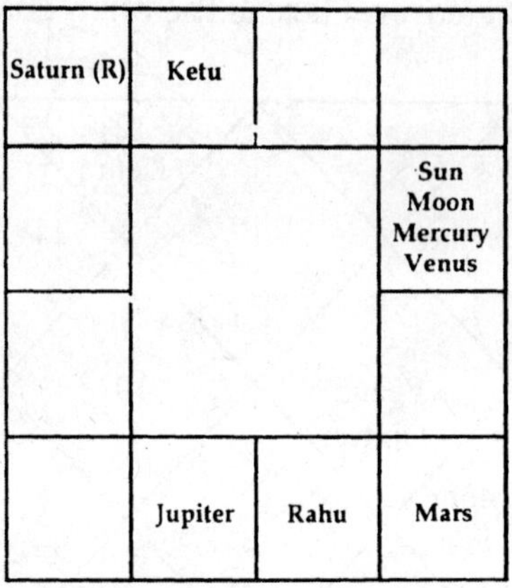

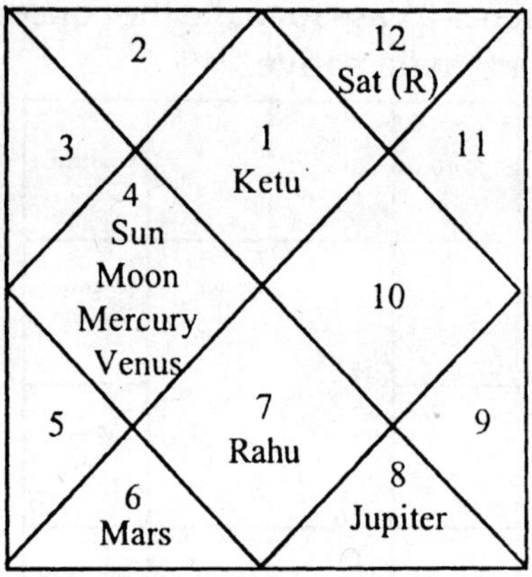

Here houses 6 and 8 are both occupied. They have secretly inimical aspect or effects upon each other. In other words the hidden circumstances are going to play important role.

It has been stated else where that when Sun and Mercury join together in any house they do not affect the relations of the native or the commodities of the planets but native's own life and comforts. The one thing that the chart, therefore, indicates is that the native's life and comforts are going to be affected. House No.6 is occupied by Mars who is an enemy of Mercury the lord of the house. This will spoil the results of the house where Mercury the 6th lord is posited. This is the 4th house. The house can be afflicted and harmed because the 4th lord Moon occupies the quadrangular house, be it his own house. Sun and Moon both are involved in the 4th house. The affliction to heart is but obvious. As the 11th house is unoccupied, the heart is not likely to get any help at the time of need.

Houses 2, 6, 8 and 12 are mutually related. House 2 aspects house 6 which in turn aspects and affects the results of 8 and 12. House No.2 is not occupied by any planet. Hence house No. 12 will not be able to pass its venom to house 2 but the house shall remain afflicted. Planets in houses 6 and 8 are both inimical to Saturn occupying house No. 2. The cause of the malefic nature of 8th house will be known by the 4th house. Thus house No.4 is the main culprit. The vulnerability of 4th house was judged by the birth chart. Now are the conditions ripe for the exploitation of the vulnerability. The house can be affected because Moon is in the quadrangle. Because of Mars in 6 Mercury raises the accusing finger to nervous system of the heart. Moon is also afflicted because of Mercury and Venus. Moon and Venus the two female planets together in the 4th house do not affect anybody or anything else.

Now let us see the parts of body afflicted by the planets. Sun governs vitality in general, bones and the entire body. Moon rules over the heart. Mercury has domain over nervous system of the body. Venus rules the face but Venus in the 4th house is the planet of Rasiphal, that is, his effects on face can be warded off by suitable propitiation. In short we can say that the native has some troubles or acute trouble in the chest or heart. Because of the involvement of Saturn and Jupiter the trouble shall be long lasting. The native suffers from breast cancer which is malignant. She has been operated upon and it is presumed that the trouble has been thrown out but medical treatment still continues. She may not be out of the woods at least for about three years which is the duration of Venus.

8

Miscellaneous Precautions :

(Remedial Measures in Daily Life)

In a Residential house

1. If there is a deep pit near the entrance which is opened only at the time of some festivities or marriages etc. to prepare foods the same should be scratched till all the burnt clay comes out and thus burnt clay should be taken out and thrown in the running water of any river and that pit should be closed.

   Misfortunes : Whenever any child is born in such a house there will be a sudden series of mishaps and it would appear as if everything has been suddenly consigned to ashes.

2. There should be no temple (even very small for individual worships) with idols in a residential house. Keeping photos or drawings of deities on paper is not inauspicious. This is more unfortunate for the native born with Jupiter in house No. 7.

3. In some houses there is one small dark room in the end where there is no passage for air or light. Such small room should be left as such without any attempt to have windows etc. If any attempt is done to have windows or other opening misfortune will strike the residents. Such rooms do not tumble down themselves.

4. There are sometimes, if it is an old house, dark and hidden places where ornaments and money is kept secretly. Such places should never be allowed to be empty. If for some reasons there remains nothing to be kept there, some dry fruits may be kept there.
5. In some houses there is no *kachcha* (uncemented) place. In such houses Goddess Lakshmi does not reside and there is no marital happiness. In such houses articles relating to Venus should be kept.
6. In some houses there is an entrance on the southern side. Such houses are most inauspicious particularly. Even the male folks get no peace, to say the least, there. In such cases the main gate should be shifted to some other side. If for some reasons it is not possible to do so, a gallery may be formed and the main gate fixed in that gallery.

About Children, safe Delivery and Prosperity

1. From the day of conception a red thread should be tied around the arm of the pregnant woman. After the delivery of the child the thread of mother's arm should be transferred to the arm of the newly born. A new thread should also be tied around the arm of the mother. This should continue with mother and child for 18 months. This is more important in these cases where the children do not survive.
2. There should be a worship of Lord Ganesha to have good children and prosperity.
3. From one's food one should give share to cow, crow and dogs.
4. To have a safe delivery a milk pot (filled with milk) and a sugar pot (filled with sugar) should be touched by the delivering mother just before the delivery and kept at another place. It will be a safe delivery. After the delivery the milkpot with milk and sugar pot with sugar should be given to some temple. It should not be brought back. The

auspiciousness will be in direct proportion to the quality of the pots.

5. Sweet loaves of bread prepared in a Tandoor (no utensil should be used in baking) should be given to Sadhus and dogs.
6. If some body's children do not survive, the native should distribute salt and salty preparations to celebrate the birth of the child.

About Alms, Charity and works for Human service :

(Reference to charts here is strictly to birth charts and not to the progressed charts or varshaphalas.)

I. Those who have their Moon in their 6th house should not have any act of charity. They should not dig or get the wells dug for public service on their expenses. They should also not open places where the thirsty may get water to drink. If this is done there is a likelihood of the whole family tree withering away and prevailing of extreme poverty.

2. It is not wise to give in charity the things relating to the planets in exaltation or strong in their charts.
3. Those who have their Saturn in house No. 8 should not build Dharamshalas or any place where the travellers may get free staying facilities. If this is done the native may even lose his house and face critical financial position.
4. Those, who have Saturn in lagna and Jupiter in house No.5 simultaneously in the birth chart, should not give in charity the copper paisa otherwise there are likely to be chain of deaths of children.
5. If Jupiter is in house No.10 and Moon in No.4 the native should not build gurudwaras, temples etc., otherwise there would be false and baseless allegations against the native leading to legal proceedings.

6. Those who have Venus in house 9 should not fix up any scholarship to poor children or periodical financial aid to widows etc.
7. Those who have Moon in the 12th house should not open schools for free education or offer food to religious heads or religious persons. If this is done it shall have very grave consequences to the native.
8. Those who have Jupiter in house No.7 should not offer new clothes to the head or pujari of a temple.

For Adopted Children

1. The younger brother should not adopt the children of the elder brother nor should he arrange free marriage of the daughter of his elder brother. If the elder brother adopts a child of his younger brother or arranges marriage of his younger brother's daughter it will be auspicious. If bad effects of Saturn are observed the things pertaining to Saturn should be given in alms through the niece and nephew.

General advice for all

1. From one's own meals one should give something to cows, crows and dogs.
2. Having meals in the kitchen is a safeguard against the mischiefs of Rahu.
3. Sweet loaves of bread each month should be given to animals. This will save the persons from avoidable illness, quarrels and expenses.
4. Keep some water in a vessel under the bed in the night and pour it at a place where it does not become dirty. It should be poured on a tree or the plant of Tulsi.

Selection of Bridegrooms

1. The native having Saturn in 11th house is likely to desert his wife, children etc. in young age.

2. Bridegrooms having Saturn in 2nd house are inauspicious for bride's family.
3. Bridegrooms having Mercury and Rahu together in houses 3 or 8 or 9 or 12 are also not auspicious to the bride's family.
4. Bridegroom having Venus and Ketu together in lagna is likely to be impotent.
5. Bridegroom having Sun in 4th house, Saturn in 7th house, Venus in 5th house and Moon in lagna or 2nd house is also likely to be impotent.
6. Sun in 6 and Mars in 10 with the afflicted 12th house or having Moon in lagna and Jupiter in 11th house is likely to be of bad sexual habits and may destroy his wealth in that.
7. Bridegroom having Jupiter and Venus in 10th house or having Moon in lagna and Jupiter in 11th house is likely to be of bad sexual habits and may destroy his wealth in that.

Selection of Remedies

Every planet rules over a particular colour, animal and tree etc. Some difficulties arise when particular animal is ruled by one planet and his colour is ruled by a different planet. In such case difficulties arise. Dog, for instance is governed by Ketu. Black colour also comes under Ketu. So long as the dog is black we can safely take him to be an article of Ketu but if it has two colours we have to decide as to which planet is represented by it. Some hints in such cases are given below for the help of the readers.

1. The dog of black or white and black colour is governed by Ketu but that of white and red or pink colour will have the effects of Venus.
2. Buffalo is the animal ruled by Saturn. If it is pure black it is surely Saturnian, but buffalo of grey colour (something like white or *Bhuri*) will come under Sun. If a black buffalo has white spot or tilak on its forehead it shall mean the combined effect of Saturn and Moon.

3. Horse, likewise comes under Moon. If it is a black horse we can mean that Moon is eclipsed by Saturn which is against Moon. If the horse has a colour resembling yellow or pale it would mean a help extended by Jupiter to his friend Moon. It shall be auspicious during the periods of Moon and Jupiter.

Combination for Children

1. Jupiter, Sun, Venus, Mercury and Saturn all are the established planets.
2. Only Jupiter or Sun or both are established.
3. Mars is in the house of Venus or Mercury or in their houses of significations and all the aspecting houses are unoccupied.
4. Mars is Mars positive and established.
5. Mars is with Mercury, Venus or Rahu or in their houses of lordship etc. and Saturn is with Sun, Moon and Jupiter or in their houses.

Combinations for Loss of children or Difficult births

1. Venus and Mercury along with Rahu or Ketu in 7th house.
2. House No.3 or 5 or 9 is occupied by the enemy of Jupiter or Sun.
3. Mars occupies 4th house.
4. Saturn, Rahu or Ketu occupy 9th house.
5. Mercury occupies lagna or Ketu and Venus in lagna.
6. Sun in 6th house and Mars in 10th or 11th house, male children will die.

9

Some Routine Remedies of Lal Kitab

1. The results of Saturn in 6th house will be doubtful. They may be good, bad or mixed. Jupiter will not give good results at that time.

   Throwing almonds or *coconuts in the running water of a river will be helpful.*

2. Jupiter and Sun in one house and Venus in subsequent houses. The profession concerning both the planets will be beneficial.
3. When Jupiter and Saturn give bad results regarding health the service of father, if in joint family with father will be helpful. Pure gold and saffron in the house will be helpful.
4. When Jupiter and Moon give bad results regarding health or wealth or both one silver thali should be kept in the house or an empty silver vessel should be buried in one corner of the house.
5. Jupiter and Moon in 4th house are very auspicious for business or service regarding the commodities pertaining to either of the planets.
6. *Jupiter and Moon in 7th house is not a good combination.* Brokerage or trade will be auspicious as profession. Articles of Ketu should be buried under ground or tied around the neck. (*vaidurya is the stone for Ketu*).

7. *Jupiter and Moon in 11th house is also not quite auspicious.* Some financial help to daughter or father's sister or maternal uncles or to sweeperess will be helpful.
8. Jupiter and Venus in 3rd house is also inauspicious. Clay toys or spreading dust where road is under construction would be profitable profession.
9. Jupiter and Venus in 6th house is also not a good combination. To fight misfortune in this regard *some golden thing in the hair of women should always be used.*

   Jupiter and Venus will help if there is a vocation pertaining to Venus. The things may not brighten up immediately but will help in emergencies or when help is most needed.
10. Jupiter and Venus in 8th house give good results generally except in financial matters. *The profession concerning mud and dust will be helpful.* Works regarding the construction of mud houses, sale and purchase of clay toys, spreading dust on roads under construction etc. will be financially profitable.
11. Jupiter and Venus in 10th house may not give bad results regarding money matters unless the *native is a non-believer or does irreligious acts.*
12. Jupiter and Venus in 11th house. The native seeks pleasures in doing immoral or secret acts that harm his vitality etc. and may have some venereal disease. *The ash of gold or silver may be useful if taken internally under medical advice.*
13. When Jupiter and Saturn are together in the 5th house the native *should never touch wine.*
14. When Jupiter and Saturn are together the *planet aspecting them should be awakened.*
15. Whenever Jupiter and Mercury are together, no good results should be expected of Jupiter.

16. To mitigate the bad effects of Jupiter and Saturn in 2nd house the remedies for Saturn would be useful.

Important Remedies

1. In order to save oneself from the poison of houses 6 and 10 one should take the things of the planet inimical to the planet in 5th house and bury them under ground or if the native has his ancestral house the same should be kept in that house till the duration of the bad results of 8th house.
2. If Jupiter is in 10th house, Venus in 11th, Ketu in 8th and Saturn in 5th house. The dogs should be fed with flour loaves of bread. The flour should be of the weight of the son and feeding continue from 25 to 48 days.
3. If 2nd house is occupied by benefic planets and the 12th house also contains similar planets it would be beneficial to awaken the 6th house. In other words the native should serve his maternal uncles and help them or serve his own daughters and help them.
4. The planet who transits house No.6 in the annual progressed chart will cause health affliction. The relevant commodities of that planet should be given in alms and charities.
5. Mercury, Saturn and Ketu will give the results of 7th house. If they are undesirable they can be remedied. Commodities of the planets or the relative signified by them should be served.
6. When the planet in 11th house of the birth chart transits 11th house or 8th house the articles pertaining to the planet should not be purchased (new) and brought in the house and kept safely.
7. House No.9 can be awakened through the 2nd house provided houses 3 and 5 are empty.

8. If house No.10 is unoccupied the planets in the 4th house cannot give good results. Service of parents will be helpful. Ten blind persons should be fed. Money in cash to the blind persons for food would be of no avail.
9. If the planets in 8th house are inimical to planets in house 11 the native will not be benefitted by anything relating to planets in the 11th house. They will be helpful if the articles pertaining to the planet friendly to the planet in house 11 or pertaining to the planet who can change the direction of the planet in the 11th, are also purchased simultaneously. If you are purchasing a house when Saturn is in 11th house you should also bring a dog to the house. If some machines are purchased the toys for the children should also be purchased.
10. The planets in the 11th house will generally give good results when they transit house No.1. When they transit the 8th house they will give bad results. In such a case the articles of the planet in 11th house or those of his friends would be helpful provided none of the planets Rahu, Ketu and Saturn are transiting the lagna at that time. If any of these planets is in the lagna the articles pertaining to the planets in 9th house at that time would be helpful. In case the 9th house is unoccupied Jupiter's articles will be helpful.
11. Sun in the 11th house will give good results so long as the native remains religious, pious and vegetarian. If he indulges in drinking and non vegetarianism the results may be awful. He may be childless.
12. If Jupiter and Ketu are good in the chart, Moon in 11th house will give very good results at least till the mother of the native is alive.
13. If Jupiter is giving bad results according to the birth chart, at the 'time of marriage of the girl (when celebrated

according to Hindu tradition) two pieces of pure gold (of any weight but the two should be of equal weight) should be given in charity as the girl is given to the bridegroom. One of those pieces should be thrown in running water of a river and the other kept by the bride which she should not sell away but should keep with her. So long as it is with the bride there would be no bad effects of Jupiter.

If Sun is giving bad results the pieces should be of red copper. In case of such a Moon pearl (white) should be substituted for gold. If real pearl is not available, a piece of silver and water from a running river of the weight of the native should be kept in the house at the time of marriage. For Venus we substitute pearls of the curd hue. For Mars it may be red (not bright red) stone, for Mercury take diamond, for Saturn iron and steel, for Rahu the remedies of Moon given above and for Ketu take stone of two colours.

14. If houses 8 and 12 are occupied by friendly planets and house 2 is unoccupied or if houses 8 and 12 are occupied by friendly planets, house No.6 contains some benefic planet and 2nd house remains unoccupied the native will do well to go to places of worship and touching any part of his body to the deity in paying his regards. This may mean touching the feet of the deity with hands etc.

15. In case of eye troubles or to remove bad effects of Saturn throw coconuts in the running water.

16. Saturn in the 6th house will be giving good as well as bad results but it shall surely spoil the good results of Jupiter. Things pertaining to Saturn like the coconuts and almonds etc., should be thrown in the running water.

17. If Jupiter is in the lagna for generally good results the native should undertake the business or trade indicated by Moon.

For help of children undertake the vocations of Ketu. For good luck of wife the things relating to Venus will be helpful. For his own prosperity or victory in quarrels, "Sun would be helpful".

18. When Jupiter is in lagna and Saturn in the 11th house service of cow is recommended.
19. When Jupiter is in lagna and the 7th house is unoccupied vocations pertaining to Venus should be undertaken. Under this combination if the native gets a male child, or constructs a new house or if any of the blood relations of the native gets married, bad results are likely to happen. In such cases the commodities pertaining to Mars should be buried underground.
20. When Jupiter is in 2nd house and Mercury in 10th house giving bad results, remedies pertaining to Saturn should be used.
21. When Jupiter is in 2nd house and Venus and Mercury in 10th house remedies of Moon are necessary. Mercury and Saturn in 10th house giving bad results need the remedies of Jupiter.
22. When Jupiter is in 3rd house Durga Paath is always suggested.
23. When Jupiter is in 4th house sleeping or inert, that is, there is no planet in 10th house the native to have good effects of Jupiter should not allow his bare body seen by any body, that is, he should be fully dressed before other persons. He will keep on having financial stability.
24. When Jupiter is in 6th house and Ketu is badly placed the native should do the remedies of Ketu.
25. In unlucky periods when Jupiter occupies the 8th house the native should give in alms the commodities of venus or Jupiter to the places of worship.
26. When Jupiter in 10th house and Mars in 4th house the native should help or serve the relatives indicated by

Mars. He should help or at least behave respectfully with his brother. Most helpful Mantra would be Shree Ganeshaya Namah.

27. When Jupiter is in 11th house and Sun, Moon or Mars are in 5th house and give bad results the native should follow some trade or business alongwith his brother or a cousin if he has no coborn.
28. When Sun afflicts other planets the friendly planets to Sun that is Moon, Mars and Jupiter should be propitiated.
29. When Sun occupies 6th or 7th house, Mercury should be propitiated. Sometimes extinguishing the fire of the chulha (where we cook our food) by pouring milk is extremely helpful.
30. When Sun is afflicted by some other planet that planet should be propitiated.
31. When Sun is in 2nd house and 8th house is vacant the commodities pertaining to Sun and the 2nd house will be beneficial. Sun alone in 2nd house will not give good effects on thing and relation pertaining to Venus.
32. Sun in house 2 will bring ill effects on female folks like sisters, mother, aunts, Bhabhis (brother's wife). They will need the remedies of Saturn. Charity of almonds and coconut oil should be given to the temples or places of worship.
33. When Sun is in 4th house his friends in 10th and enemies in the 5th house the results will be bad even though Moon himself is in 5th house. In such cases remedies of Mars will be helpful.
34. Sun's effects will be bad when Sun occupies the 4th house, Rahu as a malefic and Jupiter and Saturn are in houses 10 and lagna respectively.
    (a) In case of malefic Rahu the gifts or presents from in-laws will be harmful if they relate to the planets Rahu, Ketu or Saturn.

(b) To ward off the ill effects of Saturn help of Moon or remedies of Moon should be undertaken.

(c) To ward off the effects of Negative Mars the native should undertake the remedies of Sun.

35. Sun in 6. When he starts affecting the relatives or articles of Ketu like children and maternal uncles the remedies of Sun should be started. The best remedies would be giving gur (jaggery) to monkeys and feeding white ants with wheat or bajra. When the ill effects are on the articles (lifeless things) pertaining to Ketu the propitiation of .Mercury would be essential. To nullify the bad effects of Sun himself keeping a pet horse or keeping water of rivers or silver in the house would be necessary.

36. Sun in 6th house and 3rd house unoccupied may bring troubles in service or business or career. Feeding of dog in the temple or anywhere else will be helpful. When Mars happens to be in 10th house and Sun is in 6th there will be trouble to children. Remedies: The articles of Moon should be kept under pillow in the night and they should be freely distributed to the people on the following morning.

37. When Sun is in 7th house, following things should be kept in mind:

(a) There should be no misbehaviour.

(b) If Saturn transits the lagna, Moon will be helpless. Remedy: The fire of the chulha, where food is cooked, should be extinguished by throwing milk. This should be done after dinner in the night or evening. There should be no fire in the same chulha till next dawn. If it is very necessary to start it the same should be done at a different place.

(c) During general bad condition Mercury should be propitiated.

(d) When ill effects are felt on children or family or financial position copper pieces (square) should be buried under ground; or taking some sweets and drinking water before starting for work would be helpful. The things having colour of Venus (curd white) will be inauspicious. Colour of Saturn would be auspicious.

Apart from the above it would be better to drop some part of food in fire of the chulha before taking would be helpful. This should be continued.

38. Sun in 9th house with Mercury or Mercury in houses 3 or 5. There will be bad effects of Sun. Big old vessels of *Peetal* in the house will ward off the bad effects of Mercury.

39. When Saturn aspects Sun and some bad results of Sun are in evidence the native should reach the southern wall of his residence and stand erect facing east and bury an earthen pitcher filled with water on his right hand side with a precaution that the water of the pitcher does not get dried up during the first 40-42 days. This will give good results.

    The results of Saturn will be the same if Saturn is in earlier houses than the house of Sun.

40. (a) Touching the feet of elderly persons and obtaining their blessings always helps to increase good effects of Moon.

    (b) Selling the things of Moon (selling milk or curd etc.) will adversely affect the family members.

    (c) Keeping in house the articles of Moon (silver, rice etc.) will always be helpful in increasing good effects of Moon.

41. When Moon is inert particularly when 7th house is unoccupied we should try to activise him before 24th year of age by keeping a pet cow or a maid servant in the house. Failing this Moon in the 25 years will be bad. For this we have to bury the articles of Mars under ground.

42. When Moon in 4th house starts giving bad results (Mercury in No.3 and Jupiter in 9) the native should give green colour cloth to the girls for 43 days.

43. To propitiate Moon (of 3rd house) charity of articles concerning Moon is necessary. Mercury should also be propitiated to save money and wealth.

44. Moon in No.5 giving bad effects will be worse still if the native misbehaves or uses harsh language.

45. Moon in 5th house will be considered as sleeping if house No.9 is unoccupied. To have good effects of Moon the native should go on journey after taking sumptuous meals and also carrying some of them with him on journey.

46. When Moon in 5th house gives bad effects the person should not harm any body and if at all he has to do it he should seek the advice of somebody else. If none is available seek advice at least from the 4 walls of your own room.

47. To ward off the evil effects of Moon in 6th house it would be helpful to visit temples now and then and give in charity the articles of planets friendly to Moon that is, Jupiter, Sun and Mars. Milk should not be taken after sun-set. Curd or cheese etc can be taken after sun-set. It will be helpful also.

48. When Moon in 8th house starts giving bad results:

    (1) Bring water from the well in *Shamshan ghat* and keep it in the house for the betterment of children.

    (2) For continued good health milk should be given in charity.

    (3) Obtain the blessings of elders by touching their feet particularly when Moon is in 8th house and Jupiter in the 4th house. Washing the feet of elders and children also is helpful in bringing about good fortune.

    (4) Keeping things of Moon in the house is helpful in having long life.

49. When Mars is in 10th house giving bad results one should not take milk in the night. Even the milk cattle in the house will be harmful.

50. When Moon is in 11th house giving bad results for mother etc., the mother should wash her eyes and head with milk or giving milk in the temple of Bhairon.

51. When Moon is in 11th house and the wife of the native is about to deliver a child the mother of the native should leave the house and go somewhere else and should not see or touch the child for 43 days of its birth.

52. When Moon is in the 11th house giving bad results in respect of the mother of the native, 121 pedas which is enough for 11 persons' meals should be given to children. If there is any objection to the prospective recipients those pedas should be thrown in river or in the running water.

53. When Moon of 12th house in the birth chart transits the lagna or the 12th house again will give very bad effects. The help of Jupiter or the remedies of Jupiter will be helpful. Visiting temples of and on will be helpful.

54. Venus in 4th house stipulates two marriages. To avoid this the same couple should have two marriages with themselves and observe full formalities and religious customs etc twice.

55. For the health of the women who have been married twice by the same person the things relating to Mars and the relations shall be helpful.

56. Venus in 4th house may make the native amorous and of bad character in respect of Women. In such cases the maternal uncles will suffer most. They may have no child or they may suffer otherwise also. In such a case the remedies of Moon will be useful. Otherwise the articles of Jupiter should be dropped in the well.

57. When Venus is in 5th house and Moon gives bad results remedies of Moon will be helpful. Service of cow and mother

will help prosperity. For keeping better health private parts should be washed with milk.

58. The native, male or female, who has Venus in the 6th house should not marry the person who has no brother and sister.

59. (a) Venus with any planet, except Mars and Jupiter, in 6th house and 2nd house unoccupied is not a good omen. Solid silver in the house will be auspicious.

    (b) Wife of the native should not remain barefooted. She should wear socks so that the soles of her feet do not touch the ground.

    (c) Wife of the native should have gold in her hair. This will help in prosperity. Private parts should be washed with curd.

    (d) At the time of marriage of the native, whether male or female, father should give two pieces of gold (pure). It shall be auspicious.

60. Venus in 7th house and Rahu in 8th house will give bad effects. Lady should not wear black or blue colours.

61. (a) When Venus is in 9th house pilgrimage to religious places would be helpful.

    (b) To improve finances make a hole in the tree of neem, place a square silver piece in the hole and cover it with the wood of the neem tree.

    (c) Keep in the house a mare or silver along with honey.

    (d) On Raksha Bandhan give red bangles to the sister which have silver or silvery things studded over them. This is specially advised when Saturn transits lagna or when construction of house is undertaken.

62. (a) Venus in 10th house sometimes gives bad results in respect of the birth of the child or the wife becoming very lustful. She should wash her private parts with curd.

(b) For ill health giving a cow in charity will be helpful. This will save the sick from avoidable sufferings. Either he/she will recover or die peacefully.

63. (a) Venus in 12th house may have ill effects on the health etc. of wife. Charity by wife or in her name would be helpful provided she is not a non-believer in God.

(b) The lady should bury blue flower in the evening (between sun-set and night) in an uninhabited place.

64. When Mars is Mars negative or starts giving bad results in general, ivory or things made of ivory will be useful in the house.

65. Mars in lagna and Mercury in house No.2; but houses 7, 9 and 11 unoccupied.

(a) Activise house 9 and 11 by remedies of Jupiter or keep in the house the articles of Jupiter.

(b) For house No.7 adopt the business of Venus.

(c) No company of Sadhus till the age of 39 years.

66. Mars in 3rd house starts giving bad results. Keeping ivory or ivory articles in the house would be helpful.

67. When Mars in 4th house starts giving bad results:

(a) Cleaning daily the teeth early morning,

(b) Remedies of Moon

(c) Burying an earthen pot filled with honey in the crematorium (when there are no children or the children die after birth).

(d) To avoid long illnesses or to cure them keep deer skin in the house.

(e) In the southern gate of the house if any, dig a nail of iron in the ground which should not be visible.

(f) Birds should be fed with sweet things.

(g) Keeping ivory on person.

68. Mars in 5th house may start giving bad results. This will generally happen in the night giving bad or disturbed sleep. Keep water under the bed in the night and pour it in the morning in such a way that it does not come under the feet.

69. (a) Mars in 6th house may affect the brothers of the native adversely. In such a case the brothers should either give a part of their earnings to the native or drop them in the running water.

(b) Mars may affect the birth of children etc. The occasion of birth should not be celebrated and sweets should not be distributed. Salty things should be distributed. If there is no escape from distributing sweets salt to be touched with them.

(c) For better personal and domestic life remedies of Saturn will be useful.

(d) For the help of brothers girls should be worshipped and their blessings obtained. (Worship does not mean actual worship. They may be kept happy or their feet should be washed etc).

(e) For the welfare of children remedies of Moon are advisable.

(f) Sound moral character. No wine or women.

70. (a) For bad effects of Mars in 7th house do the remedies of Saturn. Best way is to construct a small mud wall during the day and demolish it in the evening.

(b) When sister and daughter visit the house they should not go without sweets.

71. For bad effects of Mars in 12th house.

(a) To save elder brothers from the wrath of Mars the elder brothers should not use red colour or bring toys representing Mars. To grow choti on the head or wearing khaki cap or turban will be good.

(b) The elder brothers of the native should keep with them the articles of Moon like silver.

(c) Eating sweets, offering sweets to others and sweet tongue will be helpful to improve finances and life comforts.

(d) Offering sweet water (some sugar in a glass of water) to Sun in the morning.

(e) Giving articles of Mars and Mercury and Saturn to the temples in charity.

72. (a) To ward off the bad effects of Mercury in general use a steel ring without a joint.

(b) When Mercury and Ketu have any connection clean the teeth with alum and water.

(c) Giving goat in charity.

73. Saturn giving bad results while posited in 5th house should be countered by keeping in the ancestoral house the things of Sun (Gur, grey buffalo, pet monkey). Moon (Silver, rice etc) and Mars (honey, coral etc).

74. Saturn in 6th house.

(a) Coconut or almonds to be dropped in running water.

(b) Milk, to serpents for the increase of progeny.

(c) For general bad effects of Saturn in 6th house bury an earthen pot filled with mustard oil in the bed of the running river or running water. Water should flow over it and it should not be visible. This should be done in the night.

75. Saturn in 7th house

(a) Bury sugar filled in a flute in some uninhabited place (if Saturn is not inert)

(b) Bury an earthen pot filled with honey as above if Saturn is sleeping or inert.

76. Saturn in 10th house is generally not bad. If, however, he is bad remedies of Jupiter would be helpful.

77. For Rahu's bad effects in general.

(a) Remedies of silver for mental peace.

(b) Give Masoor pulse (red) to sweeper in the morning or keep on money now and then.

(c) Drop barley equal to the weight of the sick man in running water.

(d) Keep barley in the night under the bed towards pillow and throw it for animals in the morning or distribute it to the poor.

10

Hints for Prediction

We have explained almost all the basic concepts, fundamentals and assumptions needed for the analysis of the chart according to the Lal Kitab. Normally they should be enough to prepare the reader for the job. Besides all these things there remains much to be understood before actually practising the analysis. Some of these points are outlined here as an aid for success in the work.

1. Jupiter is the ruler of the 9th house, Sun of the 5th, Saturn of 10th and Mercury of the 3rd and 6th houses. All these planets are directly or indirectly related to father or father's property but if Jupiter and Sun, Jupiter and Mercury or Jupiter and Saturn occupy a house together they do not affect the father or the parents or the parental property. They may have some influence over the commodities or the professions related to them but not the relatives themselves. They merely indicate the personal life of the native or his comforts. The same shall be true if Sun and Mercury, Sun and Saturn or Mercury and Saturn occupy the same house.

2. The female planets, that is, Venus and Moon do not generally give bad results if accompanied with male planets like Sun, Mars and Jupiter. On the other hand they mostly offer good results. Mercury in company with these male planets also behaves similarly.

3. If two or more than two planets occupy the same house and are inimical they shed their enmity. This does not mean that

they become good or helpful planets. They simply do not interfere in the results of each other. In other words when there are two or more planets in one house inimical to each other we should be guided by the results of each planet and not by the combined effects.

4. If two or more planets friendly to each other occupy a house together they become greater friends and enhance the goodness of the results of each of them. They do not become neutral to each other as is the case of enemy planets.
5. Seventh house of the chart is the Pakka Ghar of Mercury. So long as Mercury is in his Pakka Ghar, Sun, Mars, Jupiter or Saturn occupying any of the Kendras or 2nd house or the 11th house will not be able to affect the health of the native.
6. If female planets, that is, Venus and Moon alongwith Saturn occupy any single house and some other planet aspects them according to the rules of aspects the aspecting planet shall get afflicted. The relations concerning the aspecting planet shall be in great trouble. The relations concerning the aspected trio shall remain safe.
7. The planet in his own house, house of exaltation, in his Pakka Ghar or in his friend's house will ordinarily give good results unless there is some other trouble to him. The planet in his house of debility or in the house of his enemy will generally give unfavourable results. An enemy planet occupying the Pakka Ghar of a planet will afflict the results of that planet's house of occupation.
8. Houses 1, 7, 11 and 8 should normally be judged together to have correct analysis. These houses have their own mutual affinities which can best be understood if we use the metaphors of Lal Kitab. Planet in lagna is the ruler and that in the 7th house his Minister or the executive. The planets in 8th house represent the eyes of the ruler and that occupying the 11th house the legs of the ruler. If there is

one planet in the lagna and more than one in the 7th house the former will not be able to govern them properly. If the planet in the 11th house is inimical to that in lagna the ruler will not be able to walk properly. His results will be afflicted. Planets in the 8th house being the eyes of the ruler will guide and control the movements of the planets in the 7th house. If the planets in lagna and the 8th house are friends the 7th house will not be able to play mischief in the execution of the orders of the ruler. Mars in the 7th house normally offers good promise for property. If simultaneously the 8th house is occupied by Mercury he will not allow Mars to give any property. Similarly if Mars occupies the 7th house and Mercury the lagna the property will remain a far fetched dream. There shall, however, be some difference in the two cases. Mars in both cases shall offer the property but Mercury in the lagna will destroy the property by the follies of the native because there Mercury represents the native. The loss of property when Mercury is in 8th house shall be due to some unforeseen circumstances. There may be thefts, mischiefs or some other unknown circumstances. Eighth house means secret channels. The native shall have no control over them.

The planets in 11th house have likewise, their own role to play. If the planets in lagna and the 11th house are friendly they shall maintain good checks on the 7th house. If they are enemies the results will be bad. If the number of planets in 7th house is less than the number in the lagna the relatives of the planets in the 7th house are likely to suffer. It may be particularly remembered that the planets in lagna aspect the planets in the 7th house. If the planets in the two houses are inimical to each other the adverse effects shall be due to native's own follies or incompetence. The planets in 8th house keep a check on the actions of the planet in the 7th house. This may not mean that the 7th house has no fair play but simply that there may be some natural causes going against the wishes of the planet in the 7th house.

According to the rules of aspects the planets in *8th* house have a back aspect on the 2nd house. In other words the planets in 8th house will affect or promote the results of 2nd house. If however, the planets in the 11th house are inimical to the planets in *8th* house they do not allow the bad effects of 8th house to be transferred to the 2nd house. As has already been explained above the 11th house planets being the legs of the ruler, the native is careful in taking action in the matter. Planets in 8th house influence the results of 2nd house directly if they are friendly in both the houses.

9. Houses 2, 8, 12, 6 and 11 should also be judged together. This is so because:

   (a) Planets in 8 have a back aspect on 2nd house and thus affect or promote the results of the later. The vice versa is not true.

   (b) The influence of aspects of planets in 8th house can be effectively countered or helped by the planets in 11th house according to their friendly or inimical nature.

   (c) The planets in house 2 aspect the planets in the 6th house. The planets in 2nd house thus influence the planets in 6th house, but those in the 6th house also do influence the affairs of the 2nd house indirectly through the agency of 8th house with which they have secret relationship.

   (d) The planets in 12th house are not directly related to planets in the 2nd house but they do influence the results of 2nd house. The two houses may be known as *Sadhu* and his *Samadhi*, Nobody knows when the Sadhu may attain his samadhi, but he is sure to get it every now and then.

   (e) House No.6 is named as Pataal Loka, a place under this world or the places of unseen forces. They influence the planets in the 8th house, the house of secrecy. In other and simpler words the planets in the two houses work with hand in gloves together. The only difference is that they create forces which are unseen. The persons committed to benefit the native disappear suddenly in such cases. It has been seen in many cases that the persons for one reason or the other could not attend their duties on a particular day on the appointed time. They were either themselves taken seriously ill suddenly or had to go out for unavoidable reasons because some of their nearest relative expired. If the planets in these houses happen to be evil they accelerate the pace of evil influences, say, ten times more. In order to safeguard the house No.2 we need the benefics in houses 2 and 12 because they also have their own secret affinities.

(f) House No.6 and 8, with mutual connivance pour their venom in house No.2 through the good offices of 11th house. If house No.2 is unoccupied there would be none to take that poison. There would be no evil effects on the house. Alternatively if the 2nd and 12th houses are occupied by benefics then also there shall be no evil effects. If somehow the native unfortunately falls a prey it shall be momentary and short timed. Sudden help from unknown quarters shall be there to set the momentum of 2nd house in order again.

(g) If the planets in houses 12 and 8 are inimical to each other the native should be advised *not to go to any place of worship*. House No.2 is known as the place of worship. The stroke of ill luck will catch hold of the native from the places of worship or temples as they are the places of secret influences.

(h) If the planets in houses 12 and 8 are mutual enemies or if there is some very good or benefic planet in 2nd house the native should visit places of worship because by doing so he will save himself from the ill strokes. He should also touch the feet of the deity if possible or put his head on the feet of deity. In short he should touch some part of his body with the deity.

10. We judge the periods of ups and downs in life, the period between the births of younger brother to the period of adulthood of the native and about one's parents etc. by judging houses 3, 11, 5, 9 and 10.

    (a) House No.3 starts its influences on the native from the date of birth of co-born brother *provided house No. 3 is occupied.* The periods shall indicate a change after the birth of the child if houses 9 and 5 are occupied by Saturn, Rahu or Ketu. No good should be expected under such circumstances. The miseries shall be aggravated if house 5 is occupied by Rahu/Ketu/ Saturn and No.8 is occupied by planet inimical to them because in such a case the planets in 11th house shall help only in the aggravation of the troubles.

    (b) If the 9th house has good planets and house No.2 is unoccupied the native is not to gain any thing from the good 9th house. The 9th house may be taken as an ocean from where the rain clouds rise and 2nd house as the big and high mountain which can stop the clouds and make them shower their grace. No planet means no mountain.

    (c) Planets in the 10th house indicate the extent of luck, good or bad, or in other words the credit he has brought with him to be utilised in his present life. House No.4 indicates the extent to which he can draw from his bank credit. One may have large balance in his account but may be restricted in operating it. If house No.4 remains unoccupied or occupied by Rahu/Ketu/Saturn the wealth or good luck promised by 10th house will be of no avail. Planets in the 4th house indicating the drawing power of the native will go waste if house

No.10 and 2 are unoccupied. Then the ocean would be dry and if at all there are some clouds there shall be no hills and mountains to stop the clouds and rob them of their moisture.

(d) If houses 3 and 9 are bad houses, house No.5 will also be bad.

(e) For obtaining good results from house No.5 the 9th house should be occupied by Sun or Moon.

(f) If house No.5 is occupied by Rahu or Ketu and their enemies are posited in the 8th house the stroke of ill luck will be severe and this shall be through the 11th house. The sufferers shall be the relatives indicated by the planets in houses 8 and 5.

(g) Under the circumstances outlined above, if house No.2 happens to be vacant the effects will be on the earnings of the native which none shall be able to help. Even the planets in 10th and 5th house will become malefics irrespective of their natural disposition.

(h) If 9th house is occupied by Sun or Moon, then Rahu or Ketu in 5th house will have no bad effects on children or the native himself.

11. Houses 2, 4 and 10 should be judged together. This would have been quite clear from the foregoing notes. In order to have a clearer picture it may be said that 9th house indicated the conditions of life before the present birth. This may in other words be taken to mean the *Sanchita Karmas* or the deeds and misdeeds for which the native has to suffer or enjoy the fruits. All these actions do not fructify at the same time. The actions the fruits of which shall have to be reaped during the present incarnation called the *Prarabdhas* are indicated by the 10th house. The effects shall be felt through the 2nd house. For the factors limiting these benefits we have to judge the 4th house. If this house is unoccupied the native shall hardly enjoy the benefits offered by houses 2

and 10. The position shall be very much like "water, water every where but not a drop to drink".

(a) The planets in 8th house if malefic, shall claim their full toll. If house No.2 has very good planets they will invite help from unseen and unknown quarters.

(b) If house No.10 is vacant the occupation of 2nd house even by very good planets will be of no avail.

(c) If houses 2 and 10 are both unoccupied the good planets in the 4th house will succeed only in getting a mirage in the desert. Hopes and ultimate disappointments shall be the luck of the native.

11

Critical appreciation

A keen study of Lal Katab would make it clear that it is essentially a book of Palmistry but, of course, with a difference. In all the books of palmistry the lines and mounts (padded portions below the fingers) have been associated with some or the other planet. There are mounts of Jupiter, Saturn, Moon, Venus etc. Besides these mounts there are lines of planets like Sun line and line of Mercury etc. No palmist has, however, gone to identify the houses of the birth chart on the palm. This is the speciality of Lal Kitab. In fact the author has tried to co-relate the readings on the palm with the readings of the birth chart. The assertion is that God has not kept any thing secret about the destiny or fate etc. of the individual. The planets, Sun, Moon and Mars etc. have full knowledge of the Providential designs and the individual is only a part of the world. Not to keep any thing secret from the individual God has written his destiny on his hands in his own language of lines and mounts etc. Those who are astrologers commune or try to commune with the planets to unravel the mystery and those who go by palmistry try to read his Will. Firman No.2 is very clear in explaining the relationship of Palmistry with Astrology.

अक्से गैबी जाहिर पहले था सितारों पर हुआ।
नक्श जिसका पीछे दुनियां के दिमागों आ हुआ।
दिमागी खानों पर असर तब हाथ की रेखा हुआ।
इल्मे ज्योतिष इस तरह पर जब सितारों से हुआ।
सीधी टेढ़ी हाथ रेखा से क्याफा चल पड़ा।

(In the first instance Providential designs were revealed to the planets which influenced the human mind. Those mental influences were transcribed on the palm by straight and curved lines. Thus on the one hand there arose astrology and on the other hand palmistry came into existence.)

The lines on the hand do change. In order to predict the events correctly we should continue to be guided by the lines at the time of consultations. To the astrologers he prescribes the annual progressed charts or the varshaphalas. Technically the change in the lines is called the *Graha Chalit* or the planetary transits. In other words our study has to be related to the palm at a particular moment of time. The arguments appear to be perfectly sound. No adverse comments may be possible. There may be some reservations regarding the astrological way the palmistry is correlated with astrology. Some of these points have already been discussed in the introduction and other parts of the book. They may, however, be treated briefly again.

It is true that in astrology it is the planet that is the source of fruits; but it is also true that the rasis are not merely the vacant spaces for the planets to move or transit. They have their own qualities and do provide certain back ground for the planets to act in a particular way. Mars in Aries is not the same as he is in Capricorn. Venus, likewise, in Pisces is different from Venus in Virgo. This is with all the planets. The Lal Kitab takes these rasis identical with the houses of the chart. The first house or the lagna in the Lal Kitab is always considered identical with the first sign of the natural Zodiac that is Aries. This assumption at this moment of time is hard to digest. It cannot be disputed that tomorrow after research we all may come round to this assertion or alternatively the Lal Kitab itself may need modifications.

The other point that needs a research is whether the planetary aspect is restricted to influence on the houses later to the house of aspecting planet. The planets in lagna influence the affairs of the 7th house, but not the vice versa. Of course there are some exceptions. This is again a principle which is difficult to agree with.

The concept of an inert or sleeping planet is yet another such point. If there is no planet in house No.10 the planet in house No.4 is rendered as a sleeping planet and is restricted in his influence. This does not stand much to reason. There is much to be studied in this respect. Unfortunately the Lal Kitab has no great following with the result that we generally do not get the chart-readings based upon these principles and therefore, naturally enough, there is no mutual discussions and transfer of ideas. With all our reservations we wish that Lal Kitab is followed by astrologers and their findings discussed freely. The palmistry and astrology both stand to gain and by this Lal Kitab may get more prominence.

There is another concept. It is to awaken a sleeping house. The house is sleeping or inert when it has no planets in it. It can be awakened by propitiation of particular planet relevant to that particular house. Propitiation has immense power and the whole concept of remedial measures is based on it; but how far the same can be effective remains to be seen.

About remedies for various ills of afflicted or malefic planets Lal Kitab is very specific that the effects of rasi planet only can be ameliorated or warded off by proper propitiation. This appears to be a sound principle. This negates the attempts for wiping out all bad effects of the planet. This is a sound principle because otherwise the destiny or fate or the fruits of Karmas becomes meaningless. In astrology also there are some restrictions in this respect. We depend there upon the aspects of Jupiter and the 9th lord. The deeds or misdeeds do have their importance in human lives and they do shape the destiny irrespective of anything else.

About the practice of remedies there are some well laid down principles. The remedies should be of two planets, namely, of the afflicted as well as the afflicting planet There are some astrologers who suggest remedies on the basis of the bad events. This is not proper. If somebody is getting bad mental effects it is not always Moon who needs treatment. There was a lady who was getting mental fits regularly. Some astrologer asked her to wear pearl. This increased the frequency as well as the intensity of the fits. She was asked to take out the pearl immediately and instead was asked to offer two flour cakes with some sweet (batasas which are the cakes of sugar) daily to cows. It is now 4 years that she has been keeping fine. The readers may well understand the difference in the two remedies. There is a treatment of Moon in both the remedies. In one we raised the power of Moon who was already affected. The result was the intensity and frequency of the trouble. In the other by feeding the cows we dispersed the bad effects and thus diffused the crisis. This point has been very well elaborated in the system of practising remedies by the Lal Kitab which is explained to some extent below.

The medicines are practised in two ways. In some cases it is laid down very clearly that the articles of the relevant planets should be brought home and kept there or worn on person. In other cases they are to be distributed to the poor or given to the temples etc. The things that are to be kept on person or in the house are defensive in the sense that they protect the native from bad effects. Those which are to be distributed are meant to disperse the effects over a larger area and thus reduce it on the native.

One thing that we admire most in the Lal Kitab is that it is a champion of Vedic culture and philosophy. At many places it has been advised as a remedy to live in a joint family and if for some reason, due to employment and service etc, it is not possible to do so the native should sleep on the bedsheet which was used by his father. In other cases the native has been asked to obtain the blessings of his parents and elders etc as a cover or an amulet against the evil. It may be added here that such innocent remedies have really worked miracles.

The Lal Kitab has almost been quite exhaustive in the method of practising the remedies. We all believe that going to temples and offering worships is always a good thing and should be commended and encouraged. This is not so according to the book. In some cases it lays down specifically that the native should not visit the places of worship and this has its own justifications. In some cases the native may go to the places of worship and may even bow to the deity, but he should not touch any part of his body with the deity.

There is an assumption that the planet gives the result of his house of occupation and house of lordship. In accordance with the principles of Lal Kitab any planet can be asked to give the results of the house of our choice by suitable remedies. If Sun, for example, is occupying house No.3 he will give the results of 1st house because of his Pakka Ghar or house of signification, house No.5 his own house and house No.3 the house of his occupation. We can get the results of 2nd house from Sun if we keep the articles of Sun in a temple. This is quite strange. This way we can get the best results of the planets whenever we want. This has nothing to do with planetary occupation or lordship etc. This is too hard to swallow.

It would be seen from the above that there are many points which claim our admiration and there are simultaneously many other points which have no explanation. This is not to say that Lal Kitab is worth the waste paper basket. *This* is also not to say that it expounds a philosophy which should strictly be followed without prejudice or slightest deviation. What is stressed here is the need of more work and more research on its findings. The learned practitioners should come out with their experiences etc. As on date we admire the book for its remedial measures.

There appears to be a need of caution even in the practice of remedies. We may go by its remedies only if we practice it strictly accordingly to its concept, principles and theories. According to astrologers Venus in Pisces (not in the 12th house of the chart) gets exalted. We *should not jntermingle the remedies of* **LAL KITAB** *with those of general astrology,.* ***LAL KITAB*** *has its own individual identity with its own fundamental principles, theory and practice, There should* be *nothing like Gandhian Socialism. The mixed concepts shall take us nowhere.*

Glossary

Agni Kund	:	Fire pot used for yajna
Akash	:	Sky
Bajra	:	Maize - a coarse grain
Bhabhi	:	Elder brother's wife
Bhairon	:	A Hindu deity
Chopad	:	An indoor game just like chess
Choti	:	A small bunch or lock of hair on the top of head
Chulha	:	Oven
Copper coin with a hole	:	A coin equal to 1 / 100 of a Rupee- it was made of copper with a hole in the centre
Daan	:	Chairty
Dargahi	:	Natural
Desi ghee	:	An edible substance prepared by heating butter.
Dharmasthana	:	Religious place
Dharmi graha	:	Religious planet.
Durga	:	A Hindu goddess
Duraga paath	:	Enchanting mantras related to goddess durga
Ganesha	:	A Hindu deity who is worshiped first of all in every auspicious ceremony to ward off obstaceles

Ganesh Chaturdashi	: Day of Lord Ganesha
Garuda purana	: A book dedicated to the great bird Garuda, who carries god Visnu on its back
Graha	: Planet
Gur	: Jaggery
Gurudwara	: Place of worship for Sikhs
Hakeem	: Unani physician
Haldi	: Turmeric
Hari	: One of the trinity gods of Hindus
Harivanshapurana	: A book of hymns in prayer of Hari
Hanuman	: Monkey god devotee of Shri Rama
Jiva	: Living being
Kachchi	: unbaked
Kanyadan	: To give a virgin girl in marriage
Karmic	: Theory of Karma (actions deeds)
Kauri	: Tiny white shels used to play chopad
Keekar	: A thorny tree with tiny leaves - generally found in desert lands
Kesar tilak	: Mark of saffron paste on forehead
Lakshmi	: Goddess of wealth
Loka	: World
Mala	: Garland
Mantras	: Verses, generally in Sanskrit language showing mystic influence if enchanted in proper prescribed way
Masoor	: Name of a cereal used as pulse

Maya	: Things of worldly attachment
Mooli	: A root-vegetable white in colour and salty in taste.
Moong	: A cereal of green colour generally used in the form of pulse
Nalla	: Wide and shallow drain of water - it may be clean to dirty
Neem	: A big tree with long and narrow green leaves, bitter in taste
Paise	: A copper coin equal to 1/100 of a Rupee in value
Pakka ghar	: Well built house made of baked bricks, stone, cement of iron
Pap	: Sin
Papi	: Sinner
Para loka	: Heaven to hell, which is abode of soul after the death of human body
Peda	: A sweet made from milk-roast and sugar
Peepal	: A big shadowy tree. It has long and broad leaves with a tail. It is held as sacred tree. Hindus worship peepal
Peetal	: An alloy of copper and zinc
Prasad	: Some edible given to the devotees in temple as the deity's blessing
Pujari	: Priest of Hindu temple, who performs pooja (worship) every morning and evening
Raksha bandhan	: A brother-sister Hindu festival celebrated on the last day of Shravana which is the fifth month of Hindu calendar

Rin pitri	: Curse of Parents
Saathi	: Companion
Sadhu	: Saint or hermit
Saraswati	: Goddess of learning in Hindu mythology
Samadhi	: Structure raised on the grave or cremation site in honour of a deceased peron
Sanchita Karmas	: Actions or deeds performed in previous incarnation and are yet to be rewared
Saunf	: Name of a spice
Shamashan ghat	: Cremation ground
Shri Ganesh namah	: A book containing the synonyms of the name of Lord Ganesha
Tandoor	: A special kind of oven used to bake chapaties
Thali	: A circular utensil used like a plate to eat food
Til	: Sesame
Tilak	: A smearing mark on forehead made with some scented substance
Tulsi	: A small herbal plant. It is worshiped by Hindus
Vaidurya	: Cat's Eye
Yoga drishti	: Vision acquired by practising yoga.